Literacy Skill Development for Students with Special Learning Needs:
A Strength-Based Approach

by
Leslie Todd Broun
&
Patricia Oelwein

DUDE PUBLISHING
A Division of
National Professional Resources, Inc.
Port Chester, New York

Publisher's Cataloging-in-Publication
(Provided by Quality Books, Inc.)

Brown, Leslie Todd.
    Literacy skill development for students with special
learning needs : a strength-based approach / by Leslie
Todd Brown & Patricia Oelwein.
        p. cm.
    Includes bibliographical references.
    ISBN-13: 978-1-934032-07-7
    ISBN-10: 1-934032-07-7

    1. Reading—Remedial teaching. 2. Children with
disabilities—Education. 3. Individualized instruction.
    I. Oelwein, Patricia L. II. Title.

    LB1050.5.B76 2007   372.43
                                   QBI07-600104

Acquisitions Editor: Helene M. Hanson
Associate Editor: Lisa L. Hanson
Production Editor, Cover Design: Andrea Cerone
National Professional Resources, Inc., Port Chester, NY

Dude Publishing
A Division of National Professional Resources, Inc.
25 South Regent Street
Port Chester, New York 10573
Toll free: (800) 453-7461
Phone: (914) 937-8879

Visit our web site: www.NPRinc.com

Printed in the United States of America

ISBN 978-1-934032-07-7

<u>Acknowledgments: Leslie Broun</u>

First, I would like to thank Patricia Oelwein for her first book, *Teaching Reading to Children with Down Syndrome*. Patricia's work enabled me to discover the learning potential of so many students with Autism Spectrum Disorders and Down syndrome by providing a viable means of teaching them how to read. She has been a wise and generous mentor.

I thank those teachers and teaching assistants in the Peel District School Board in Mississanga, Ontario, who worked with me as we implemented the methodology. I owe particular thanks to Lynn Butlin, Maureen Hughes and Cathy Morello who, in the early days, drove with me through more than one snowstorm to give workshops. I thank Carol Herbert, Angie DiProspero, Donna Daigle Benoit, Tej Persaud, Sandy Caves, Margit Angove, Laurie Conkie-Feitor, and Lesley Fleming-Scott for their imagination, creativity, and perseverance in teaching their students to read, as well as all of the other teachers and teaching assistants who were willing to take a chance with something a little different.

I thank the Geneva Centre for Autism, not only for their ongoing international leadership in disseminating knowledge and research on Autism Spectrum Disorders, but also for having given me opportunities to give many workshops and presentations on literacy skill development to parents and teachers.

I am very grateful to Maureen Bennie, the director of Autism Awareness Centre Inc., who has sent me all over Canada to give workshops on the development of literacy skills. She contributes significantly to the world of ASD in Canada.

Patricia and I would like to thank Robert and Helene Hanson for giving us the opportunity to write this book and share this information with others. They have graciously led us through each stage of the process. We would especially like to acknowledge the significant contribution of Lisa Hanson in her editing of our manuscript. Her work has been insightful, precise and her clarity of vision has guided us throughout the creation of this book.

Finally, we thank all of the students with whom we have had the privilege and pleasure of working. They have enriched our lives beyond measure.

Acknowledgments: Patricia Oelwein

A special acknowledgment goes to Leslie Broun, the primary author, for conceiving and initiating the writing and publication of this book. During her years of dedicated service to students with learning differences, she has constantly sought effective methods to meet their special learning needs. Having found the method that has been most effective, she has refined and expanded it to include children with autism spectrum disorders and is now sharing her wealth of knowledge. This gift will truly make a difference in the lives of students, their families, and their educators.

Also, I would like to acknowledge Abby Rusin and her family for sharing their photographs for the picture cards, and to Alison Weinberg, my daughter, for her word family illustrations.

Table of Contents

PREFACE

By Patricia Oelwein

Reading is a skill most of us take for granted, but it does not come easily for many students with special needs. Because of difficulties with perception, cognition, and speech, children with Down syndrome, autism, and other developmental disabilities face huge challenges in acquiring literacy skills. Many of these children never learn to read or write because they cannot master the prerequisite skills (Koppenhauer et al., 1991).

Yet young people with special needs must acquire literacy skills, and educators can effectively teach these skills provided they understand how to teach to students' strengths. The field-tested method presented in this book will train teachers to teach literacy skills to a wide range of students, many of whom have traditionally not been expected to read. Very often, understanding the printed word can prompt verbal language; by learning to read, many children who aren't able to verbalize spontaneously or engage in conversation also learn to speak (Sundberg & Partington, 2000).

For typical students, reading is usually taught through a phonics-based, "bottom up" approach in which they learn to recognize words by sounding out letters and syllables. Special learners often need a different approach. The method presented in this book teaches to the strengths of special needs students by initially emphasizing the visual recognition of words. The method uses a "match, select, and name" sequence to prompt sight recognition, and guides students through specific stages of learning with each set of words taught. As students learn to recognize whole words by sight, they move into sentence building activities and reading short books that have been individually created for them. Throughout, the emphasis is on acquiring new skills through a structured process of practice to fluency, transfer, and generalization that builds on what students have previously learned.

This method, systematically applied, assures initial success in reading and enhances both verbal and written communication skills. Over the last 30 years, this approach has been used in 39 states and the District of Columbia, as well as 14 foreign countries.

The inspiration for this program was Dennis, a four-year-old boy who, in 1972, was enrolled in the Program for Children with Down syndrome at the University of Washington in Seattle. He was a delightful little boy who did not speak. Valentine Dmitriev, the coordinator of the program, asked me to help foster Dennis's communication skills by teaching him to read.

My method of choice was the match, select, and name process, in which the young person matches written words on flashcards to pictures representing the words, selects words on verbal cue, and says or signs the words as he reads them on flashcards. This is the foundation of the Oelwein method.

I chose words for Dennis based on what was most meaningful and useful to him, starting with *Mommy, Daddy, Dennis*, and *Eric* (his brother's name). When these words were mastered, we moved on to animals, a subject in which Dennis had shown a strong interest. Dennis readily learned to match and select these words, but naming—the verbal response to the word—was slow in coming. He acquired visual language before verbal language; however, he did start to speak. The breakthrough occurred one day when I told him to select the word *Dennis*. Instead, he grabbed the flashcard with his brother's name on it and stated emphatically, "Eric!" When we added sign language to name the words as Dennis read them, his progress in speaking soon equaled his matching and selecting skills. His verbal responses increased dramatically when tubes were put in his ears to aid his hearing.

Dennis's success in reading and speaking was impressive, and learning to read became part of the program's preschool curriculum. Observation booths made it possible for university students, trainees, parents, and visitors to observe young pupils making substantial progress in all areas of development; however, their achievements in reading received the most attention. When this first class of students went to kindergarten, they demonstrated that children with Down syndrome could not only learn to read, but could also learn to comprehend what they were reading, as well as improve their speaking skills.

Two years after Dennis had his first lesson, data from his kindergarten class showed that five children in the Oelwein sight reading program had a mean of 52.6 words (range 40-62) in their reading vocabulary and were reading books for beginning readers. A psychologist who tested one of these pupils, five-year-old Joy, reported that she was reading at a second grade level. Since then, teachers have successfully used this methods not only with students who have Down syndrome, but also with many other students who have special learning needs.

Initially, we didn't know why this method worked; we just knew it did. Now, with advances in educational and medical research, we understand more about how the brain receives information and why special learners benefit from the visual, systematic, and strength-based instruction that this reading program provides.

The Oelwein method has been replicated internationally, beginning in 1975 at Macquarie University, North Ryde, NSW, Australia, and most recently at the Al Nahda Model Schools (specializing in Down syndrome) in Riyadh, Saudi Arabia. Developing the Al Nahda program was daunting. Our consulting team had to work through interpreters. The trainees took endless notes, and these were virtually the only learning materials they had. Yet we were able to develop a specialized and systematic reading program, spanning from infancy to age 21, that is now being replicated in the public schools in Riyadh.

One Al Nahda teacher was particularly skeptical about our approach. Nevertheless, she excelled in applying and extending the methodology with her students during the two years she taught at the school. She left to become the principal at another school, where she trained all the teachers in our method. She told them they were required to try it for just three weeks and, after that, were free to go back to their old ways of teaching. Not one teacher has done so.

Leslie Broun, who in 1996 was a special programs resource teacher in the Peel District School Board in Ontario, Canada, wrote to me after using the methods in my book, *Teaching Reading to Children with Down Syndrome: A Guide for Parents and Teachers* (1995). She stated that her students who had Down syndrome were making such remarkable progress in reading that she thought that we should "reevaluate how we classify these children as developmentally disabled." Leslie eventually adapted and expanded the program to teach reading to students with Autism Spectrum Disorder and other disabilities.

We have written this book, incorporating Leslie's modifications, so that an even wider range of students can benefit from its proven approaches. We hope you find as much success and fulfillment as we've experienced using this method to develop literacy skills in students with special learning needs.

INTRODUCTION

By Leslie Todd Broun

For seven years, I taught a self-contained class of children with Autism Spectrum Disorder. These students were at the more severe end of the spectrum, and our primary goal was to help them develop skills in communication, behavior, social interaction, play, and self-care. While some of our students eventually progressed to working on academic skills, this was not the primary focus of the program.

Years later, when I began working as a resource teacher for students with developmental disabilities in mainstreamed classes, I quickly realized that I needed to find or develop strategies for teaching reading, mathematics, social studies, science, and other academic subjects to my students. The problem was that truly effective strategies for teaching these skills to children with special needs were in short supply.

My role was to facilitate a positive inclusionary experience for all. To do that, I had to provide the teaching staff with strategies that were truly useful and applicable to each child, and I shared the frustration of teachers and teaching assistants who had few tools at their disposal. How could we meet students' special learning needs in the regular classroom? What materials should we use? What would they look like?

Some children with special needs were able to learn with simple modifications to the curriculum. Others struggled as we tried to provide materials that were interesting and varied. Although I was constantly reading and researching, I hadn't found a teaching method that truly met the needs of these young people.

Then, in the fall of 1995, I heard about a new book by Patricia Oelwein, *Teaching Reading to Children with Down Syndrome: A Guide for Parents and Teachers*. As I read it from cover to cover, the realization dawned on me that Patricia offered a definitive and sequential process for teaching reading, along with reinforcement activities and extensions that could meet the needs of many of my students.

At that time I had a caseload of 36 students, 12 of whom had Down syndrome. It was an ideal situation for performing my own controlled study. Over the Christmas holidays, I prepared a kit for each student containing everything that would be needed to initiate the learning process—a synopsis of the methodology, word grids, flashcards, a scrapbook, and a blank book.

In January, 1996, I held a workshop for the teachers and teaching assistants of the 12 students with Down syndrome (and was delighted that some of the parents also came). I introduced the methodology, emphasizing that we would start with vocabulary words that were meaningful to the students. By the end of the workshop everyone knew what to do and agreed not to make any changes to the teaching procedure, a critical component in doing a comparative study, even for an informal one such as ours.

Within days I was receiving ecstatic phone calls from instructors: "Leslie, you won't believe it, he's reading four words! Eight words! He's reading sentences!" They could barely believe how well and how easily their students were learning to recognize words. The students were engaged and happy to come to the worktable. The phone calls continued.

Several things were happening:
- The teachers and teaching assistants were excited because they were able to see progress and skill development as a direct result of their work. There is nothing more thrilling than seeing tangible learning take place, particularly with special learners.
- The students understood that they were participating in "real reading" and were proud of their efforts.
- The classmates of students with Down syndrome were changing their ideas about the special needs students' ability to learn and take part in the regular academic program.

These students continued to show steady progress in developing reading skills. It became commonplace for them to take turns reading to the class. This facilitated a greater level of classroom inclusion and enabled students with special needs to be perceived as learners.

As my caseload grew, so did the number of my students with Autism Spectrum Disorder (ASD). More information was becoming available about the visual learning style of children with ASD, and I decided to try Oelwein's sight word recognition methodology with these students. I was nervous, yet hopeful. As I traveled from school to school, I introduced and demonstrated the methodology, and I was not disappointed. Teaching reading to these students presented challenges, but with a few accommodations, many students, including those for whom literacy had not previously been considered a possibility, were able to develop reading skills. When students realized they could be successful, they came readily to the table to learn.

Over the next few years, by persevering with the Oelwein approach to sight word acquisition skills and its extensions (which this book describes in detail), I was able to learn a great deal about how the reading process works for students with ASD. I now speculate that the power of this methodology is perhaps even more significant for children who have ASD than for children who have Down syndrome (DS) or other developmental disorders.

Most children with DS are quite socially inclined and communicate more easily than children with autism. Although they may struggle with some of the physical aspects of speech production, as well as with difficulties caused by hearing loss and/or cognitive disability, children with DS generally understand how language (both verbal and non-verbal) is used in social communication. Children with autism, on the other hand, have significant difficulties with communication and social interaction. Enabling students with ASD to organize language for communication through the reading process has emerged as the most significant benefit of using this methodology.

As a result of this success, many teachers have approached me about using the Oelwein method as an intervention for neurotypical* students who have significant reading difficulties. Often, these students have little or no phonological awareness, are unable to combine sounds efficiently, and have extreme difficulty using a phonics-based approach to developing skills in reading. They are, however, able to respond to the Oelwein systematic whole word approach and perceive words as units of sound and meaning. With time and experience, it became obvious that all children have different learning needs and that one size—one method—does not fit all. In acknowledging differences in learning style, teaching must reflect an understanding of this differentiation.

The goal of this book is to provide the instructor with strength-based strategies to build skills in the following areas:
- Sight word recognition;
- Alphabet and phonics;
- Word families;
- Spelling;
- Grammar and sentence construction;
- Reading comprehension;
- Printing/writing/keyboarding;
- Composition and creative writing.

These skills reflect a progression of development and participation in literacy. Students who have special learning needs will often require a specialized approach that teaches to their strengths. Indeed, their literacy skill development program may look quite different from that of their neurotypical peers; however, the goals are the same. The approach is simply individualized for the student's particular learning style.

This book provides teachers not only with the pedagogical rationale for using the Oelwein method for the development of word recognition skills, but also with explicit direction for the instructional steps to be taken and the kinds of visual materials that can be created and used to build skills.

---

* The term "neurotypical" refers to individuals who do not have neurological differences that cause a particular disorder, such as autism.

Developing the understanding that an orthographic "picture" is representative of persons, places, ideas, and movements is both incredibly sophisticated and, at the same time, very simple. Through the Oelwein method, students learn that these "pictures," or symbols (words), represent Mommy, Daddy, Grandma, a favorite pet or story character, in a way that teaches to their strength in visual learning.

The first stage of this approach involves students acquiring personalized sight word vocabularies. Students work to accumulate and add to their collection of sight words. However this is only the beginning! An ever-growing stack of flashcards is not an end in itself; rather, it is the first step in enabling students to understand that words in their printed form have meaning and that these words can be manipulated to share thoughts, create messages, and participate in classroom literacy-based activities in a meaningful way.

The skills of matching, selecting, and naming are the critical building blocks of acquiring a sight word vocabulary. In this three-part process, not only are students' visual skills engaged, but also their kinesthetic (i.e., the physical act of matching a word to another word or to a picture), auditory and digital (speaking/signing) skills. Students usually progress quickly to the selection stage, where they are able to select words on request. In the naming stage, students are able to either say or sign the word, as well as demonstrate comprehension by placing the word on the appropriate picture (although this task can eventually be eliminated as a student's general comprehension improves).

As students develop confidence in recognizing their individualized sight vocabularies, they move forward through the processes of learning to create sentences, read stories, and further develop their decoding skills. It is our hope that teachers, paraprofessionals, parents, and other concerned educators will find the information in this book to be useful and easily applied. The goal of special education is to provide instruction that is meaningful, relevant, and effective. With this book, we have provided a "tool kit" of literacy strategies to do just that.

PART I

WORDS

CHAPTER ONE:
A STRENGTH-BASED APPROACH

The Framework: Universal Design for Learning

The Oelwein method for the development of literacy skills in students with special learning needs is framed in the principles of **Universal Design for Learning** (UDL). The Council for Exceptional Children (2005) states that the three basic tenets of UDL are the use of a curriculum that:
- Represents information in multiple formats and media,
- Provides multiple pathways for students to respond and express themselves,
- Provides multiple ways to engage students' interests and motivation.

Throughout this book, we discuss ways and means of engaging students in literacy, first using subject matter that is personal and relevant to their own lives, and then extending outwards to the greater environment. For students with learning difficulties and developmental disabilities, participation in literacy allows for greater participation in the curriculum. Our goal is to make learning accessible to these students, and learning to read is a key feature of participation, not only in school, but also throughout life.

Key features of UDL include:
- *Learning is an active process: Learning is personal because it begins with individuals.* The approach to literacy skill development presented in this book begins with the life of the child; materials are chosen that are relevant and meaningful to the individual student.
- *Instruction is engaging: Lessons are structured to involve students' natural thinking processes and interests.* The Oelwein method is geared specifically to the visual learning style that is the strength of many students with Autism Spectrum Disorder, Down syndrome, and learning disabilities who have difficulty with auditory learning processes.

- *Instruction is individualized: Students will understand the world from their own unique vantage points.* Students are engaged in direct instruction that exactly meets their style of learning. The use of content that is personal for the individual student encourages participation.

Another key feature of UDL is that subject content and skill work is structured to be accessible to the learner; as such, it is set at the student's level of ability, yet is challenging enough to be motivating (Vygotsky's Zone of Proximal Development). In working with students who have developmental disabilities, accessibility may also mean certain physical accommodations, such as the use of materials that are large and strong enough to withstand repeated usage. The use of motivating content, materials, and a methodology that facilitates accessibility of learning, eliminates much frustration. Behavioral issues are minimized as the student willingly comes to the table to engage in tasks.

The Oelwein method also builds on the educational applications of Universal Design for Learning, as cited in *Universal Design for Learning: A Guide for Teachers and Education Professionals* (2005):

1) Equitable curriculum: The Oelwein method allows students to access the development of literacy skills across the curriculum.
2) Flexible curriculum: This method allows teachers to modify content and elicits meaningful student participation.
3) Simple and intuitive instruction: The Oelwein method provides a straightforward means of instruction for students with developmental disabilities who are visual learners.
4) Multiple means of presentation: This method calls for presenting material in a way that meets the needs of students who have developmental disabilities and are visual learners.
5) Success-oriented curriculum: Student success is paramount. All instruction is geared toward enabling students to learn effectively and efficiently.
6) Appropriate level of student effort: This method stresses ease of access to content through visual supports and varied means of student output, including hand signs, pointing, and the use of assistive technology (computer hardware and software, as well as voice output devices where applicable).
7) Appropriate environment for learning: organization of the learning space is addressed with emphasis on the physical and visual aspects of organization.

It is essential to keep these applications of Universal Design for Learning in mind when working with all students, particularly those who have learning difficulties. By making skill development and subject content as accessible as possible, students are set up for greater success.

The incorporation of new ideas and methods into daily instruction can sometimes be daunting, especially in this time of rapid communication and intense educational and medical research. The strategies presented in this book are framed within the tenets of Universal Design for Learning, making them accessible, useful and relevant to teachers and their students.

Literacy Skill Development for Diverse Learners

"Educators limit future opportunities if they make an a priori assumption not to teach reading to some students because of the nature or severity of disability" (Browder, D. et al., 2006, p. 393).

Reading is a subject that needs no promotion. No one has to be sold on the merits of teaching reading to typical children. However, this is not the case for many children who have learning differences. Those opposed to teaching reading to students who have developmental disabilities argue that it is a waste of time because these students don't understand what they read, and it isn't really reading if it is not phonics-based.

In reconsidering our expectations for literacy skill development, we need to liberate students with learning differences from traditional reading measurements and methods, where the desired outcome is proficiency in technical reading skills. Traditionally, **vertical goals** are set for higher grade-level scores. Using this model, students may experience failure, and in some cases, failure results in termination of reading instruction. Even if a student does not fail and is able to attain higher levels of reading skills, this approach may not be beneficial to the child if the grade level for reading is considerably higher than the child's level of comprehension.

Instead of **vertical goals** for attaining higher levels of reading skills, students should have **horizontal goals** that expand on how they use and enjoy reading. Horizontal expansion of reading skills has an ongoing effect on communication and on building competencies that lead to independence and success in a range of situations. As students apply reading to communication, social skills, school subjects, and recreational reading, reading grade level will gradually increase, but this increase is not the measure of reading success (Oelwein, 2002).

"If teachers dismiss the literacy ladder and adopt the 'web model,' students won't need to acquire a certain skill set before being invited to participate in the curriculum and instruction in general education classrooms; learners won't be expected to develop, behave, and learn in the same ways; and individual differences in learning will be supported and appreciated" (Kluth, 2003, p. 139).

Autism Spectrum Disorder

Many students with Autism Spectrum Disorder (ASD) have difficulty learning to read through the development of phonemic awareness and phonics skills. This difficulty may actually have a genetic origin, as reported by Dr. Fred Volkmar of Yale University. At the Geneva Center International Symposium on Autism in 1998, Dr. Volkmar explained that persons with ASD usually have irregularities on the following chromosomes:

- Chromosome 1: responsible for phonemic decoding, and phonics
- Chromosome 6: responsible for phonemic awareness
- Chromosome 15: responsible for single word segmentation

In 2002, Dr. Roberto Tuchman reported irregularities on the following chromosomes of persons with ASD:

- Chromosome 7: oromotor skills (initiating and coordinating the movements of the mouth)
  - verbal dyspraxia: difficulty with the production of words and sounds
  - phonology: understanding the sound system of letters
  - syntax: understanding how words are combined to make meaning
  - motor dyspraxia: difficulty with initiating and coordinating movement
- Chromosome 15: cognition and motor skills

> **The Genetic Factor:**
>
> Many students with autism may be genetically predisposed to having significant difficulty in learning to read using a phonics or sound-based approach.

Understanding that there may be a genetic explanation for the difficulties many students with ASD have with instruction that is sound-based or auditory makes it clear that educators need to offer these students a viable alternative for developing literacy skills. The Oelwein method's whole word sight recognition approach to initiating the reading process provides this alternative.

Many children with ASD are able to learn the alphabet and sound/symbol associations with ease, however the application of this knowledge can be problematic. Some students may become efficient phonetic decoders and be able to follow a traditional path in developing literacy skills; however others, while knowing the letters and their sounds, will not be able to apply and blend them efficiently. During the oral reading process, words are pronounced in a choppy, letter-by-letter fashion. This can produce significant frustration and difficulty as so many words in the English language are irregular in their spelling. Some students who are particularly rigid in their habits continue the process of decoding words letter by letter despite rehearsal and repetition because that is the way the word was learned and therefore this is the process that "must" occur. For these students, it is often necessary to re-teach using a whole word approach in order to correct the letter by letter pronunciation ("c-a-t" versus "cat").

Children who are verbal and who speak intelligibly are usually able to learn to read using a sound-based approach; however, children who are non-verbal, who have emergent verbal skills, or who are echolalic (repeat words, phrases, sentences, and even long passages of speech), tend to have most success with a whole word sight approach to reading. In general, a dual approach, starting with teaching whole word sight recognition followed by introducing phonics-based instruction, has been found to be the most effective way of teaching reading.

Down Syndrome

Modern technology has made it possible to study the brain through magnetic resonance imaging. Wang (1996) reports the results of a study that found actual physical characteristics in the brains of adolescents with Down syndrome (DS) that explain weaknesses in verbal tasks and verbal short-term memory skills and relative strength in visual-motor skills. This medical and educational research should guide educators when planning and implementing education plans for these very special children.

It is sometimes assumed that students with Down syndrome are incapable of participating in the process of developing literacy skills. Currently, it is estimated that 60% of individuals with Down syndrome are illiterate (Fowler, et al., 1995). Parents of children with Down syndrome offer a variety of explanations for their child's illiteracy, such as:
- "He never learned the alphabet (never passed the readiness test);"
- "She tried, but failed (she just didn't get it);"
- "He read when he was in elementary school, but instruction was discontinued because he did not seem to be making progress;"
- "She did not test high enough to learn to read."

The reasons given for not teaching reading to students with Down syndrome do not stand up to a more accurate understanding of the learning potential of this population. Encouragingly, it is never too late for an individual to begin the process of learning to read.

> The oldest person with Down syndrome who I taught to read using the method presented in this book was 42 years old. Although he had been considered incapable of learning to read, he learned the skill quickly and was thrilled with his achievement. — P. Oelwein

Teachers and instructors must consider the quality of their students' lives as well as their futures when making decisions regarding whether or not to teach them skills in literacy. Think of what it would be like to go through life and not be able to read: never to have a text book, never to write things down, never to be able to look up information you forget, or to read a greeting card, menu, bus schedule, or TV guide. Imagine being expected to remember and learn everything from verbal instruction when short-term auditory memory and auditory processing is compromised.

Using the Oelwein method, countless students with Down syndrome have proven capable of learning to read, and often thrive in the subject. Some students can learn to read in traditional reading programs; however, for others, the match, select, and name method is the best way to learn to read early and successfully. For some students, starting with this method prepares them for moving on to traditional methods.

A remarkable characteristic of persons who have Down syndrome is that they generally read at higher levels than expected based on cognitive scores obtained from standardized tests. This "over achievement" is observed when comparing general ability age (K-ABC scores) and age-equivalent scores for word attack skills, word identification, and comprehension. Data for 33 young adults (17-25 years of age) with Down syndrome showed that age-equivalent reading scores exceeded general ability scores, the greatest mean difference being in word identification (2.6 years), the least mean difference being in comprehension (one year) (Fowler, et al., 1995).

The Issue of the "Plateau"

A school psychologist was appalled when a mother, whose son was 16 years old requested that reading goals be included in his IEP. He told her that her request was ridiculous, because he had tested her son, whose IQ was 36 and who was reading at a first grade level, and he only qualified for vocational training.

The mother reasoned that if the psychologist's testing was accurate, it demonstrated that the student was reading above his mental age of 5.8 years (first grade reading age equivalent is between 6 and 7 years). Reading should, therefore, be included in his IEP; however, he should not be taught at a first grade level with a reading goal of reading at the second grade level. Rather, his reading goals should be to apply his existing reading skills—and expand on them—to build his competencies and independence on the job and off, in each environment. First grade reading goes a long way when reading and following schedules (school, training, and bus) and directions, as well as reading the name of the bank where he will be depositing his checks. — P. Oelwein

Educators and parents often express concern that students with Down syndrome hit a learning "plateau." The students appear to stop making progress in reading at a certain point, often around the second or third grade. This may represent a period of consolidation rather than an end to the learning process. During this period of time, students' scores on standardized reading tests bear little relevance to the value reading has for them. It is reading itself that is valuable, regardless of the reading level. Once students have moved into the world of the literate, reading will serve them well, as long as the reading material is at their level. In addition, when used, reading skills continue to develop during adulthood. Learning is a lifetime activity for all, including people with Down syndrome. It doesn't fully plateau; it usually progresses in a gradual incline, not easily detected by standard measures.

Kliewer (1998) followed ten students with Down syndrome in inclusive classroom settings for two years. He observed that it was teachers' attitudes, rather than student performance, that determined whether or not students were included in regular classrooms. Teachers for whom higher reading scores were the *end product* excluded students with Down syndrome, and other children in the class who were not meeting expectations, from full curricular participation. However, teachers who viewed reading as "the construction of shared meaning in specific context," where the *end product* was not only improved skill in reading, but also in communication, fully included *all* students in the curriculum.

General Learning Disabilities

Many students have significant difficulty with auditory processing and the development of phonemic awareness skills. For these students, a traditional and typical phonological approach to the development of reading skills may not be sufficient. Students may languish for several years trying in vain to develop sound/symbol associations and apply them to rapid and efficient decoding.

> Mary, a student with Down syndrome, was a fairly fluent reader and she derived tremendous pleasure from reading. Fellow student Lisa had been diagnosed as being learning disabled and had no reading skills whatsoever. She was noticeably upset at listening to her table partner, Mary, read and being unable to do so herself. I asked their teacher if I could try the sight word method with Lisa and she agreed. I quickly made two grids and eight flashcards and asked Lisa what words she would like to learn to read. She gave me a list and we set about the **match, select, and name** process. Within minutes, Lisa could recognize the words and make short sentences with them. Not only that, but Mary, who had also been participating in the process, could also read them. It was agreed that the girls would be reading partners and that they would learn words together. In fact, Mary became not only Lisa's reading partner, but also a reading teacher. Lisa's final comment to me that day was, "These are the first words I've ever been able to read." That made my day. — L. Broun

The effect of learning to read on self-esteem is immeasurable, especially for students who have experienced difficulty over a long period of time and who have come to believe, as a result of their ongoing inability to utilize the phonemic decoding system, that they would never learn this important skill.

Another occasion particularly stands out in my memory involved a group of four boys in the second grade (two for whom English was not their first language) who had not been able to develop decoding skills through the traditional approach. I employed the Oelwein approach with them, first asking them what words they wanted to lean and then taking them through the match, select, and name process. They were amazed to see one another recognize the four words with ease. After they had learned both their words and their peers' words, I added a new grid for all of them that included the words: *I, and, like* and *the*. With the addition of these new words, they were all able to create short sentences and read them. I was later told that the boy who was most enthusiastic through-out the process and who wanted to be first to make a sentence was the most recalcitrant student in his class. The entire process of working with these four students took approximately 25 minutes, during which each of them learned from 12 to 20 words. While review and reinforcement would be necessary for retention and generalization, this was an excellent starting point for teaching reading to typical students who were not able to participate effectively in a traditional phonics-based program. — L. Broun

Students who are Deaf or Hard of Hearing

As the Oelwein method is geared to visual learners, it is particularly useful for students who are deaf or hard of hearing and do not have auditory access to the sound/symbol system. For these students, this approach to word recognition provides an efficient tool that allows immediate access to active participation in literacy.

One size does not fit all:
Teachers must remain open to new and different methodologies.

Sometimes we have to think outside the box!

A Strength-Based Approach

Most people take the skill of reading for granted. Learning to read is simply part of the school experience, and it enables participation in all other aspects of schooling and of life. For students with special learning needs, however, the ability to read does not usually come easily. Because of difficulties with perception, cognition, and speech production, many students may not be able to participate in the traditional phonics-based approach to developing reading skills, which in turn negatively affects them in a variety of ways.

> **How do we define "reading"?**
>
> **Is reading the process of letter by letter decoding?**
>
> or
>
> **Is reading the derivation of meaning from print?**
>
> Webster's dictionary defines reading as "to look at so as to understand the meaning of something written or printed." The journey by which we reach this state of being able to read may differ from one individual to another. We cannot confuse process with outcome.
>
> ***To read is to derive meaning from print.***

Reading is essential to many areas of life and learning. Consider the following:

- Reading conveys information and interpretations about the immediate environment.
- Reading provides a visual translation of expectations, thereby helping individuals understand how to navigate an environment and be independent.
- The written word provides a visual means to assist with organizing internal thought and expressing thought.
- Subject-focused word recognition allows for more meaningful participation in the curriculum. Students are able to learn crucial vocabulary words and apply even rudimentary reading skills to subject areas other than just language arts/English.
- With the acquisition of reading skills, students' self-confidence improves. Aware that they are learning and demonstrating an important skill, students are proud of their accomplishments.
- As more vocabulary is acquired through reading, students may become able to expand their internal language for thought and communication.
- The development of reading skills may significantly improve an individual's ability to participate in the workplace.

> Learning to read allows individuals with special needs to transition from the world of the illiterate to the world of the literate, thereby affecting entire lives.

The Limitations of a Phonics-Based Approach

In special education classes, students are often expected to master prerequisite skills before they are considered ready for reading instruction; consequently, many children are never taught to read and write because they are unable to master the prerequisite skills. (Koppenhauer et al., 1991). The current approach to reading instruction typically considers learning the alphabet, the sequence of the letters, and sound/symbol associations to be the necessary prerequisite skills for learning to read. Many neurotypical students who are able to master these skills have success with learning to read through a phonics-based decoding approach, understanding sound/symbol associations fairly quickly. With sufficient practice, these students are able to sound out words and understand the text that they are reading.

The learning style of children with a variety of special learning needs (such as students who have Autism Spectrum Disorders, students who have Down syndrome, students who are deaf or hard of hearing, and students with certain expressions of learning disability) makes it difficult for them to learn through a phonics-based approach. For these students, the letter-by-letter decoding of words is a labor-intensive process that can be both frustrating and discouraging. Many children with special learning needs, or those who may not be able to respond to an auditory approach to learning, are instructed via a sound-based approach for many years, yet they never actually develop the ability to read. While they may learn to sound out words slowly and laboriously, their speed and skill level may never allow them to derive meaning from print in an effective or enjoyable manner. The auditory learning approach and subsequent expectations for decoding are neither efficient nor effective for these students.

> "Poor readers are often inefficient because they have been taught to look too carefully at each word...Slow reading results in poor comprehension because the reader is so focused on individual words that he forgets what came before and has to re-read" (Goodman, 1995, p. 26).
>
> Is a sound-based instructional process effective for students who struggle with learning to read? Can or should another approach be considered for teaching these students?
>
> **Do not persist with a "longer, harder and louder" sound-based approach if the student is not meeting with success within a reasonable time frame.**

Strength in the visual modality

Crucial to the pedagogy of teaching students with Autism Spectrum Disorders, Down syndrome, and learning disabilities is the understanding that many of these students are primarily **visual learners** (Kluth, 2003; Janzen, 2004; Hodgdon, 1995; Grandin, 1995; Quill, 2000).

> Quill (2000) reports that research has found that individuals with ASD process visuospatial information more easily than transient auditory information. Information presented in a visual format can be attended to or looked at for as long as necessary while auditory input must be encoded instantly.

As opposed to the traditional "bottom-up" phonics-based (auditory) approach to reading, the Oelwein whole word approach teaches to the strength of students who are visual learners. Not only does the Oelwein method access the **visual** learning modality, the other three learning styles (auditory, kinesthetic, digital/spoken) are also engaged:

- The spoken word is heard (**auditory**) when it is paired with the printed word.
- The physical matching and selecting processes, as well as the construction of sentences using flashcards, addresses the **kinesthetic** component. For students who use hand signs, the kinesthetic component is further engaged.
- Students who have verbal skills are able to engage the **spoken** element of participation in literacy as they read aloud, offer answers and respond to the teacher's questions. For some children, the ability to participate verbally is an emerging or developing skill. For students who are non-verbal, the use of hand signs can be encouraged to enable the student to participate in literacy skill building activities.

It is important to clarify that this whole word sight approach to teaching reading *does not exclude* the development of phonemic awareness skills or an understanding of the use of phonics for decoding; rather, adjusting teaching to meet the visual learning needs of students who struggle with traditional sound-based approaches teaches to the strength of the child.

A Strength-based Alternative

A Top-down Approach

Many children with Autism Spectrum Disorders and Down syndrome (or other developmental disabilities where auditory processing is compromised) will find it easier and more efficient to learn to read by first recognizing **whole words**, and then working backward from the whole word to the sounds contained within words. For many students who have special needs, learning the letters and their sounds is initially too abstract. Letters are not perceived as the building blocks of words, they are simply perceived as single units that have no meaning.

> **Point of interest**: In a recent study (Koshino, 2004), MRI brain scans revealed that when performing letter recognition tasks, the right hemisphere (the part of the brain that processes shapes) was activated in individuals with autism. The imaging data indicated that the participants with autism, while knowing the names of the letters, remembered them as shapes, while the control group of neurotypical learners remembered letters by their names (in the left hemisphere of the brain).

For students who recognize letters and know their sounds, a laborious process of integrating sounds while decoding text may significantly compromise comprehension of what they are reading. Once students experience success with reading words and simple sentences, a combination of both sight and sound/symbol association is optimal, however visual learning will remain the primary learning mode for most students with ASD.

The use of personal and meaningful vocabulary

It is critical that reading material be relevant to students' own experiences. One of the keys to the success of the Oelwein method is that the vocabulary used to introduce the concept of reading is **meaningful to the child**. It is important that students buy into reading and become "hooked" on the process. The names of family members, pets, favorite foods, toys, places, TV shows and characters and other special interests all serve as excellent sources for building vocabulary. Students have an immediate use for the words taught: to talk about their special interests and be able to ask for access to them, either verbally, through sign, or through print. For students who have limited verbal skills, the use of personal, relevant vocabulary enables not only ongoing reinforcement, but may also increase the likelihood that these words will be added to spoken vocabulary. Along with topical vocabulary, sentence building words (such as *I, see, like, the, here, is, my*, etc.) must also be taught in order to facilitate sentence construction.

Systematic instruction

Focus on the desired outcome: students will be able to read to the best of their ability and use words to frame and communicate thoughts.

As discussed in the introduction, the development of literacy skills is based on the principles of systematic, sequential instruction that requires tracking, record-keeping, and ongoing assessment. An organized approach is necessary if students are to develop an understanding of how to use words to frame and communicate thoughts. The methodology is straightforward: this is a wheel that does not have to be re-invented. The core sequence to this strength-based approach is comprised of three steps:

1) **Matching:** the student matches word to word (or word to a word printed under a picture);
2) **Selecting:** the student selects a word upon request;
3) **Naming:** the student names the word on request, either verbally or by hand sign.

This methodology employs a systematic problem-solving format that is used in developing Individualized Education Plans (IEPs) and group lesson plans. It involves:
- **Assessment** of abilities and needs: identifying areas of need;
- **Goals and objectives:** determining the desired outcome;
- **Planning and preparation:** developing lesson plans and materials to meet the objectives;

- **Implementation:** teaching according to the plans;
- **Evaluation:** determining the effectiveness of the teaching;
- **Moving forward:** an ongoing systematic process with new objectives, based on evaluation, building on previously learned material, the students' interests, and what is meaningful and useful to them.

Summary:

When teaching reading to students with special learning needs, it is important to remember the essential purpose of reading: to derive meaning from print. Instructors must ensure that students are engaged in a way that allows them to experience success quickly. For students who struggle with the traditional auditory or sound-based approach, a viable alternative is the use of a strength-based methodology that teaches to the visual learning style. Through the development of whole word sight recognition skills and the acquisition of a sight vocabulary, students are able to participate in reading quickly and successfully. Key elements in this process include the use of personal and meaningful vocabulary and a systematic approach to instruction that involves the key sequence of matching, selecting and naming.

2

CHAPTER TWO:
A SPECIALIZED METHOD
FOR SPECIALIZED LEARNERS

The strength-based approach to teaching reading at the core of the Oelwein method makes reading feasible for visual learners who do not thrive with traditional approaches to literacy. Time and resources are not lost on teaching skills that are meaningless to these students, nor are students made to continue with instruction that is not helping them to progress. Also, and importantly, time and resources are not expended dealing with challenging behaviors that may result from trying to make learners conform to methods that do not respect their learning differences, and ignore their strengths.

Careful programming that guides students through the learning process is at the core of the Oelwein method. It is critical for teachers to understand:
- the **learning process** and its application to visual learners;
- the **stages of learning** and the importance of taking the student through each stage.

<u>The Learning Process</u>

The six main elements of the learning process are: exposure to the environment, sensory input, perception, processing, demonstration of learning, and feedback.

1) Exposure to the environment:
Everything is new to infants and young children as they experience the world for the first time. They see, hear, taste, touch, and feel, but are not able to discriminate. They are not able to make meaning of their world. The people in their lives (usually parents) help children interact with the environment and give meaning to it so that they can understand how things work, the correlation of cause and effect, sequence of events, classifications,

and strategies for organizing this information, as well as labels for what they see, hear, taste, touch, and feel. They also need stimulation (experience in and interaction with the environment) to learn language and understand how to use it to communicate.

Children with learning differences and impairments may have difficulty learning to communicate through the natural exchange between parent and child. Specific kinds of interaction, including taking turns, playing, singing, talking, and reading to children, prepares them for developing skills in literacy. The more thoroughly prepared they are for reading, the more readily they will learn.

Although students with special needs may be very delayed in their ability to communicate and may not meet the usual criteria for reading readiness, they have learned more from their environment than they are able to communicate. If they have basic table readiness skills and are able to match, they should be able to learn to read using the Oelwein method, the core of which is careful programming that takes the learner though the learning process.

2) Sensory Input:

Neurotypical children take in sensory input, perceive its meaning, process it, and then store it in their short-term memory instantaneously. If this information is used and rehearsed often enough, it goes into the long-term memory where it is filed away for quick retrieval and future output anytime it is needed.

Children with learning differences and impairments are often unable to absorb information from the environment as readily as neurotypical children. They may filter out much of the sensory input in their environment because it is too much, too fast, and/or too confusing. The amount of sensory input and the rate at which it is presented need to be regulated to match a student's ability to absorb, perceive and process. In addition, the sensory input should be clear, simple, and meaningful to the student.

Children who have weaknesses in their short-term auditory memories have relative strength in their short-term visual memories. The spoken word lasts but an instant. The written word, picture, or illustration can remain for as long as necessary to be perceived and processed. For this reason, it is important to pair **visual** input with auditory input; without this component, very little learning may take place.

3) Perception:

Perception refers to the learner's understanding of perceived information. It is important for the teacher to know that the learner's perception is accurate.

A teacher told me the following story of an error in **perception** that occurred when she was attempting to teach her student, Claire, her colors:

I began the lesson on colors by cutting out squares from orange construction paper (visual input), and took Claire through the match, select, and name process, first asking her to put orange on orange (match), then asking her to show me orange (select), then holding up an orange square and asking her to name it. Claire successfully completed the exercise, correctly matching, selecting, and naming "orange." Shortly after the color lesson, Claire was working on a natural wood form puzzle. I picked up the square block and asked, "What's this?" Claire smiled and answered with confidence, "Orange!"

The student had remembered the word from the color lesson, but she had mistakenly perceived the word "orange" as referring to the shape. She had heard the word "orange," paired with seeing the orange square, and she processed the information by matching, selecting, and naming, and filing it in her shape file. Her response during the color lesson had been correct, and her teacher had given her positive feedback, telling her she was correct. Not until she asked Claire to name the square did the teacher realize that Claire received the wrong message. The sensory input for the color lesson was flawed, leading to an error in perception. — P. Oelwein

In the above-cited example, the teacher made the assumption that Claire would perceive and understand the variable that was being requested: color or shape. Instead, Claire was not able to discern what the teacher actually wanted and offered the answer that was most recent in her task memory, illustrating the importance of making very clear what is being taught and what is being evaluated.

4) Processing:
Neurotypical individuals generally have a mental "filing system" in which information is stored for easy retrieval later on. However, many students with ASD and other developmental disabilities may not have files. Instead, they have a bucket into which information flows as it comes and is all mixed together in no particular order. For these students, files need to be created to replace that bucket. The input must be presented in the context of how it is used and to which category it belongs so that it can be stored, retrieved, and used. The choice of what information to put in the file is most important as well: It should be information for which the learner has an immediate and ongoing use, and should be presented through the stages of learning—acquisition, practice to proficiency/fluency, transfer, and generalization.

5) Demonstration of Learning:

After information has been processed, pondered, and filed, the learner needs to have an effective means of demonstrating or communicating that he has comprehended, perceived and processed information. The means of demonstration will depend on the abilities and skills of the learner and will vary with the situation (individual or group instruction), but output is a very important part of the learning process. Without demonstration, it is impossible to know whether learning has taken place. This was the case with Claire, who mistakenly understood that "orange" referred to a shape. Demonstration is essential in determining when objectives have been met.

The most typical form of demonstration is either verbal or signed language: students tell what they have learned by saying words and answering questions. In contrast, visual learners often are unable to use verbal language to confirm what they've learned. They must have time and opportunity to adequately process information in order to be successful in demonstrating what they have learned, either verbally, with sign language, or through gesture, such as pointing. Also, students should be proficient in matching and selecting before they are required to give a verbal or signed response.

- **Non-verbal demonstration:** Claire **matches** the flashcards, *Claire, Mommy, Daddy*, and *Sam* to the same words on picture cards. Claire **selects** (gives, takes, or points to) these words on verbal cue.
- **Verbal (or gestural) demonstration:** Claire **names** (say or sign) the words as she reads them on flashcards.

6) Feedback:

Students must know whether their responses/demonstrations are correct or incorrect. Without accurate feedback, the learning process is incomplete. For visual learners, feedback can be verbal, visual and/or tangible. Providing students with tokens or stickers that they can use to chart their own data, measure their own progress, and set their own goals, allows them to fully participate in the learning process and evaluate their own performance.

Note: Food is not recommended as a reinforcer for the process of learning to read. In general, it has been found that success in acquiring new words or reading a passage in a special book may be intrinsically rewarding to many students. While reading is a behavior that should be encouraged, it should not be imbued with expectations for other non-academic behaviors.

The Stages of Learning

In order for basic literacy skills to become a permanent part of their repertoire, students must progress through all four stages of learning: **acquisition, fluency, transfer,** and **generalization**. These stages often overlap, but for clarity, they will be discussed separately.

1) Acquisition: During this stage students acquire new vocabulary or object recognition using the **match, select**, and **name** sequence.
- **Match:** This is the simplest skill. Students match to a sample and **hear** the teacher name it. They have to look for the word that is the same and think, ponder, and process the information as they match. The teacher gives feedback.
- **Select:** Having successfully matched, students are asked to select (on verbal cue) from multiple choices. To select, they have to remember the name of the requested word or object and select it. At this point, the teacher may guide the child's hand to the correct choice saying, "There, you found it."
- **Name:** Students have to say or sign the name of the word or object. In addition to remembering the name, they have to give a spontaneous verbal or signed response. The teacher gives feedback as to whether or not the response is correct.

2) Fluency: Fluency refers to the rate of correct response (word identification). After meeting the acquisition stage objective, students need opportunities to review and reinforce their skills until they are proficient or fluent. The teacher provides practice during the teaching session, as well as during other activities. Motor-planning issues and retrieval skills will affect some students' daily fluency rate. Because of this, a student's ability to perform the task may fluctuate and it is important to note any factors that may influence day by day performance.

3) Transfer: At this stage, in the case of word recognition, students are able to recognize words presented on different colors of paper, in different fonts, and in different contexts. Review and reinforcement activities are planned so that students can transfer the use of their skills to other activities, materials, and situations.

4) Generalization: Students are able to use the information or skill whenever and wherever the opportunity arises. It is sometimes necessary for adults to embed extra opportunities for students to use what they have learned during the daily routine to assure that they continue to use it.

Assessment

Before beginning a new initiative, it is worthwhile to examine and analyze the learning behaviors exhibited by a student and what skills he or she brings to the learning situation. This kind of analysis and assessment can expose potential areas of weakness and enable the teacher to problem-solve before the student experiences difficulty, thus leading to student success and a positive attitude toward the learning process.

Assessment is an ongoing component of the educational experience. This may be formal assessment using standardized tests, or the informal use of regular classroom probes and tests, portfolios, functional behavior assessments (either for behavior or for learning goals) and other evaluative instruments, such as the Brigance Inventory of Early Development. Ideally, parents and teachers share their observations and the results of assessments. To assess the student prior to commencing instruction, consider the following:

- What academic skills does the student already have?
- How does the student perform specific tasks: assisted, supervised, or independently?
- What skills does the student need to better function in his environment?
- What medical problems might the student have that would interfere with learning?
- What strengths does the student have that would facilitate learning?
- Does the student have difficulties for which accommodations must be made?
- Priorities—what does the student need to learn?

When learning a new skill such as reading, problems may arise as students progress through the stages of learning. If this occurs, review the steps that have been taken to determine the starting point and exact nature of the difficulty. Circumstances can usually be altered to enable instruction to continue. Sometimes, a cause or solution is not immediately clear, in which case it can be very useful to invite a colleague to observe the student who is struggling during the instructional period, or have the colleague review the student's materials and records. The perspective of another member of the teaching team can often pinpoint and clarify the nature of a difficulty.

Ongoing assessment and precise documentation of each student's progress is essential throughout the learning process. These enable the teacher to plan for next steps and accurately report on the student's learning goals in his Individual Education Plan.

Goal Setting: Integrating Literacy Skills into Functional Domains

After careful observation and sharing of information, it is essential to develop goals for the student within each domain. Functional domains include self-management, social interaction, communication, leisure, and vocational skills. Applied academic domains include reading, writing, spelling, math, science, and social studies. Literacy goals may be included in the functional domains. For example:

- **Self-management domain**: A student who needs assistance to move from one activity to another may have a goal of reading and following the classroom schedule independently. If he has difficulty controlling his behavior, his goal may be to read and follow the classroom rules.
- **Social domain**: A student who does not call his parents, teachers, and classmates by name may have a goal of reading these names and using them during social

interaction and conversation. If he does not play games, a goal may be to read and follow game directions and play the games.

- **Communication domain:** If the student does not speak in sentences, a goal may be to read simple sentences that relate to his experiences and speak in sentences during conversations. If he does not participate in conversation, a goal may be to read scripts and use them in conversation.
- **Leisure domain:** A student who is dependent on others to operate entertainment equipment may have a goal of reading and following directions for operating the equipment, reading the names of his favorite CDs, selecting his preferences, playing them, and putting them away when finished. Reading for pleasure is always a goal as well.
- **Vocational domain:** A goal may be for the student to read directions for performing the steps of a work-related task or read directions for how to reach a place of work.

After goals have been established, objectives for meeting each goal are documented. These objectives state what the student must do to demonstrate achievement of the goals. Objectives are written in measurable terms.

Planning

Now that the groundwork has been laid, the next step is to develop lesson plans to meet the desired outcomes and to implement the necessary plans. Lesson plans are the teacher's guidelines for meeting the objectives. A lesson plan states:
- **Objectives:** what the student is expected to be able to do;
- **Materials:** what the teacher prepares and/or organizes for the lesson;
- **Procedures:** how the teacher implements the lesson to draw out the best in the student.

Implementation

As teachers become proficient in following these guidelines, the procedures will become routine. The guidelines can then be adapted to fit individual teaching styles and apply unique, creative ideas to work materials.

To maximize effectiveness, teachers should:
- Follow the **match, select, and name** sequence;
- Teach with constant awareness of the stages of the learning process;
- Expand teaching to include all stages of learning;
- Differentiate teaching from testing;
- Differentiate exposure from systematic teaching;
- Expect and wait for the student to respond.

Evaluation

It is important that performance be documented to determine student progress, as well as to evaluate the effectiveness of the teaching. Record data to determine:
- When each task in the **acquisition stage** has been mastered;
- When **fluency** has been reached;
- When the student has **transferred** and **generalized** the use of words;
- When to go to the next step—**keep the learning process moving**;
- When **each objective has been met**;
- Words that **need more practice**;
- The **rate of learning**;
- Whether there is **progress**, **no progress**, or **regression**.

It is important for students to play an active role in their own evaluations so that they are fully aware of what they are learning and the progress they are making. This is achieved by:
- **Charting** daily performance: Students can participating by counting the numbers of flashcards they were able to identify, the number of sentences they read, or the number of the pages in a book that they read. These results can be charted on a bar graph or simply recorded on a calendar. Results can be charted over time to provide students with a visual record of their progress.
- **Comparing** each day's performance to the previous day's to indicate progress: "I read two more words today."
- **Evaluating** performance: "I read the most words on Thursday."
- **Setting goals:** "Tomorrow I will read three more words."

When evaluating a student's ability to participate, it is always critical to ask oneself: What is being assessed in this situation? One must peel away all of the extraneous factors and evaluate only the expression of the requested and required skill.

Do & Don't List

- **Do** help students discriminate between words they know and words they don't know. When a student misses a word when reading, unobtrusively correct the child with simple comments such as, "Try that again."
- **Do** make a note of words missed, and provide more practice with these words.
- **Do** individually review the data with students: "You missed these words yesterday. Let's practice so you can get them right today."
- **Do** teach students to ask what a word is, or say "help me" when they don't recognize the word. Praise them for asking for help.
- **Don't** start a teaching session with "What is…?" This is the test. Teach first, then test.
- **Don't** allow students to get into the habit of guessing or mumbling something unintelligible when they don't know a word.

- **Don't** request that students "sound it out" if they don't have the skills for phonemic decoding. This interferes with comprehension and puts students on the spot, increasing anxiety and making reading unpleasant and undesirable.

Move Forward

It's important to keep moving forward, taking students through the stages of learning and building on each set of words they learn so as to increase vocabulary and the ability to read the words in sentences, as well as to maintain their interest in the process.

This is a language experience program—the words that are learned must be within the students' experiences and interests, so that they have an ongoing use for reading and speaking these words frequently. Start by teaching students their names, the names of close siblings, and the words *Mom* and *Dad*. Move forward by using these names in games and simple sentences, which will be compiled into each child's first "reader." From there, move on to another category that is meaningful, useful, and interesting to the child.

Do not make the mistake that one mother made of restricting reading to flash-cards only. This mother of a four-year-old girl with DS boasted that her daughter had learned to read the names of the seven dwarfs and everyone was amazed at this accomplishment—her proud parents, grandparents, teacher, bus driver, friends and neighbors. But now she had a problem: Her daughter had lost interest in reading the words and refused to read them. She was bored with performing her parlor trick, which was the only use she had for reading these words. When her mother was asked why she had chosen to teach her daughter those particular words, she said that her daughter liked the story *Snow White*, and that some day, when she learned to read the story, she would be able to read the names of the dwarfs.

The mother had the right idea of picking words within her daughter's interests, but these were her first words, and they are limited to one story, and the use of the words (to amaze adults) was limited as well. She was not moving on to using them in sentences. In addition, there was a big gap between reading these first words and reading the story—the reader needs an immediate and ongoing use for reading the words. The child was already burned out on reading flash cards, and without an ongoing use for the words, she would soon forget them. Because of burn out, she was not interested in reading new words. The goal of "amazing" the adults was accomplished, but the child was not moving forward. While the Oelwein method provides effective tools for teaching, one must exercise care not to exploit it. — P. Oelwein

The Stages of Learning — A Case Model

Task Example: Color Recognition

1) Acquisition

Objective: Claire will *match* and *select* orange and black objects, and *name* (say or sign) the color of the objects for at least 80% of trials for three consecutive days.

Claire's tasks:
- **Match:** Put the orange objects in the orange box and the black objects in the black box as the teacher names the object and color, using color as an adjective. After correctly completing this activity for 80% of trials for three days, proceed to the next step: selecting.
- **Select:** On verbal cue, take orange and black objects from a container that contains both black and orange objects. After correctly completing 80% of trials for three days, go to the next step: naming.
- **Name:** Say or sign the color of the objects spontaneously when cued: "What color is this?" Or, "The color of the pumpkin is_____." When she has correctly completed 80% of the trials for three days, the acquisition stage is complete.

2) Fluency

Objective: Claire will practice matching, selecting, sorting, and naming colors (orange and black) during teaching session, table activities, and story time.

Claire's tasks:
- Match, select, and name orange and black objects during color teaching sessions. As each new color is taught, the colors previously taught will remain among the choices and will also be practiced.
- Sort orange and black objects at the game table.
- Point to and name the colors in books and the environment.

3) Transfer

Objective: Claire will make a paper jack-o-lantern using a model, and will describe her product using color words.

Claire's tasks:
- Select orange paint.
- Paint a paper pumpkin orange.
- Select black triangles for eyes and nose, and a black crescent for the mouth.
- Paste black triangles on orange pumpkin to make a face.
- Talk about the jack-o-lantern using color words, black and orange (orange with black eyes, nose, mouth), or teacher can prompt by asking, "What color is the head?" Or, "The eyes, nose, and mouth are_____."

4) Generalization

Objective: Claire will name and use colors spontaneously as situations in the environment present the opportunity.

Claire's tasks:
- Say or sign colors words (orange and black) as used naturally during conversation, in making requests, and in joint attention activities.
- Select orange or black objects as requested: "Bring me the orange crayon."
- Use colors when playing games, selecting clothing, coloring, painting, and anytime in the natural environment when the opportunity presents itself.

Summary:

The Oelwein approach requires understanding the learning process and its relation to the development of reading skills for visual learners. The methodology is applied through the framework of systematic instruction, taking the student through the stages of learning. Two critical elements of this method are the use of relevant, meaningful, and interesting reading material, and moving forward at a rate that will allow the child to learn efficiently while maintaining interest in the process.

Using this top-down approach for building literacy skills, most students will almost immediately experience success. Once students are able to participate in reading with confidence, the more difficult aspects of decoding can be tackled; thus, phonics and spelling are approached later in the process than they would be for neurotypical learners.

Eventually, students will be working on all areas of literacy simultaneously, but in the initial stages, it is crucial that they become engaged with the act of reading – that it is perceived as an enjoyable activity in which they can be successful.

3

CHAPTER THREE:
SETTING THE STAGE FOR LEARNING

Preparation of Materials

In preparation for implementing this program, the first step is to assemble the supplies that will be needed to make materials such as picture cards, word cards, games, and books. Depending on the resources available, these can be lo- or hi-tech. The difference will be in the appearance of the materials, and, perhaps, in the time it takes to make them. It is important that materials be neat and well-organized. Useful supplies include:

- cards, approximately 5 x 8 inches (5" x 8" index cards or make from card stock)
- card stock or tag board
- scissors, paper cutter, ruler, glue or tape, stapler
- wide felt pens and fine point markers
- laminator (if a school laminator is not available, many of the large stationary stores sell small, portable laminators at a reasonable price)
- photographs/line drawings
- paper
- zip-lock freezer bags for storage of materials
- digital camera
- computer
- book binding machine

Start-up Materials:

- **Picture cards:** Cards that show a picture with the word printed under it.
  - ○ **Glue or tape photos** of family members on 5" x 8" cards, leaving about 2 inches at the bottom of the card for the word.
  - ○ **Print the name** of the person in the photograph in the space under the photo using black felt pen.
    - ▸ Print letters approximately ¾ inch high or 48 font in Ariel type style if you are using the computer.
    - ▸ Use upper- and lowercase letters appropriately.
    - ▸ Print carefully with uniform letters (block printing).
  - **3) Laminate** picture cards for durability.

- **Flashcards:** Use cards approximately 5" x 2" (See Appendix T3.1. for template).
  - ○ **Make flashcards to match** the words on the picture cards (letters should be written in the same size and in the same way on the picture card and flashcard).
  - ○ **Make two flashcards** for words such as *I* and *see*, for which there is no corresponding picture card.
  - ○ **Laminate** flashcards if necessary.

- **Book:** This can be a regular notebook with blank pages allowing for the addition of drawings or cut-out pictures. Alternatively, a book binding machine can be used to create a book of approximately 8 to 10 pages using stock paper or tag board. Pages can be 7" x 7" or 8" x 11", depending on which size will be most appropriate for the illustrations.

- **Word Grids:** The standard word grid used in the teaching process is printed on 8 ½" x 11" stock paper or tag board (See Appendix T3.2. for template). It is essential that grids and flashcards be prepared on a uniform color of paper, such as white, pale gray or blue. This provides the student with a unified visual picture without the distractions of different colors or sizes of flashcards.

These simple materials are easy to collect and prepare. Experiencing success with the program is often an inspiration for creating one's own innovative materials. Many inexpensive review and reinforcement materials have been devised that may enhance the student's program significantly.

Preparation Time and Human Resources

The time required for the initial implementation of the Oelwein method is relatively short. Two or three grids and the accompanying flashcards can be created in about ten minutes. However, creating some of the specialized materials discussed in this book can take a bit more time. Below are some practical suggestions for preparing and implementing the program:

- Have the students in another class "adopt" a student (or students) in either mainstreamed or self-contained settings for the purpose of creating their reading materials. The "adopting" students are often able to come up with new ideas and teaching tools. Participation in this kind of activity can truly draw upon the creativity of typical peers. Creating learning materials for children with special needs demands the following high standards of production:
  o Correct spelling and grammar;
  o Clarity in visual presentation: understanding the need to keep the work uncluttered and spaced in a visually attractive manner;
  o Neatness;
  o Exactitude in printing or keyboarding;
  o Precise cutting;
  o Clear and attractive art work.

- The Rainy Day Lunch Club: Similar to the suggestion above. Hold an orientation for student helpers: provide instruction for how to make materials, make clear expectations and standards of production and explain how the materials will be used. Invite students to visit the class that is using the materials so that they can see learning in action and appreciate what a valuable service they have provided.

- Parent Volunteers: Most schools are fortunate to have parent volunteers who are willing to help out in numerous ways. Again, a small group of volunteers could prepare materials for students who have special learning needs.

- Community Service: In many schools, students are required to commit a number of hours to community service. This would be an ideal opportunity for them to fulfill that requirement. It might also provide students with an opportunity to learn about children with special needs and the joy of working with them.

- Campfire Girls/Girl Guides/Scouts: Very often, youth service groups such as these are actively seeking ways of contributing to their communities. This might be a project that a group would wish to take on.

- Student Teachers: It is worthwhile, and even crucial, for student teachers to experience teaching students who have special needs and who learn in different ways. Learning how materials are constructed and applied in teaching atypical learners can provide an excellent learning opportunity for any teacher candidate.

Finally, while there is a need to create materials at the beginning of this specialized approach to reading, individualized materials are not required as students progress. Students are encouraged to move onto regular print books as soon as possible, although there is always the option of continuing to use personal books (discussed in Chapter 7) with students who struggle.

> Several years ago, I gave a workshop on reading sponsored by the Autism Society in Chatham, Ontario. At the end of the workshop, I acknowledged the aspect of the time involved in making materials and offered a few suggestions to facilitate this process. I was pleased to be invited back the following year to give another workshop.
>
> At the beginning of the second workshop, the teacher of a class of students with special needs shared her experience: Immediately after she had left my workshop the year before, she went home and called a friend of hers, a teacher on her staff who had an eighth grade class. She asked her friend if her eighth grade students could "adopt" the special needs class and help with making materials. The eighth grade teacher enthusiastically agreed.
>
> On Monday morning, the teacher went to the eighth grade class and explained the project and how the students would be involved. She showed them how to make the word grids and flashcards and how to set up the personal books. It was an ongoing effort. The students were happy to be involved and several of them expressed interest in working in the classroom with the students with special needs. The teacher taught them how to implement the Oelwein method and they accepted the challenge to help the young students with special needs develop literacy skills.
>
> The program lasted through the year and what was particularly moving was that even once the eight grade students moved on to high school, they continued to come back to visit and to see how "their" students were doing.
>
> —L. Broun

The Organization of Materials

When working with students who have special learning needs, it is critical that work materials are organized in a way that is apparent to the students. Materials should be arranged in such a way that they are readily available to the teacher and that each day's work is neat and presented in an orderly manner. There are several tools that can help with this process:

- Bins: Students need to have their own set of bins for storing their individual learning materials. There may be a bin for reading, one for mathematics, one for fine motor skill development, etc. At each student's workstation, it is also helpful to follow a structured teaching format (Mesibov & Howley, 2003) and have a "task" bin and a "finished" bin.

- Rings: Metal rings that are found in the binder section of most stationary stores are very helpful for storing and organizing flashcards. Cards can be organized alphabetically, one-hole punched in the corner, and stored on rings. For review, the student can be offered two rings and asked to choose one. Keeping the words arranged alphabetically also allows them to be quickly accessed for sentence building activities. They can also be sorted by topic or curriculum area—science words, geography words, etc.

- Bags: Zip-top sandwich and freezer bags are extremely useful for keeping materials organized. Store flashcards in sandwich bags. Word grids, flashcards, and thematic unit materials can be stored in larger zip-top freezer bags.

At the Desk or Work Table

It is important for students to be physically comfortable at the desk or table in order for them to maintain attention to the lesson. Chairs should be the correct size for the children: feet should rest on the floor with a 90 degree angle at the ankles, knees, and hips. If feet do not touch the floor, a telephone book can provide a useful footstool. The desk or table should be at a height that allows students to comfortably work on it with about a 90 degree angle at their elbows. Children with special needs frequently have motor and balance problems and need this stability so that they can focus on the lesson, and most need this structure to prepare them for the learning process. Some young children enjoy working on the floor; this position is acceptable provided it works well for the child and the teacher.

For periods of direct instruction in word recognition skills and sentence construction, as well as first efforts at reading stories, a quiet, non-distracting environment will facilitate learning. Students with demonstrated distractibility issues may benefit from withdrawal from the classroom into a seminar room or a quiet corner of the library for twenty minutes a day. Contrary to the idea that this is not inclusionary, this temporary accommodation ultimately leads to greater inclusion. Once the students with special learning needs have acquired literacy skills in a quiet environment, they can return to the regular classroom where they are able to participate meaningfully in group work and class projects.

Length of Time for Instructional Sessions

The length of time that students are able to engage in instructional sessions truly varies from student to student. At the beginning of the process of learning to match, select, and name words, some students may need sessions to be as short as three to five minutes at a time. For other students, fifteen minutes may be possible. The crucial factor is that, regardless of ability to sustain attention, students are positively engaged in this process. Students should leave the table feeling that they have participated in a task that they have been able to perform well.

Don't be concerned if initial periods of instruction need to be brief. It is more important for students to be successful and leave the table in a positive frame of mind than for them to sit at the table for a specific length of time. The goal is for students to develop positive associations with participating in literacy skill development activities so that they will come to the table readily, anticipating the enjoyment and the feeling of accomplishment that they will experience.

As students gain more sight word recognition skills and move on to sentence building activities and reading short books that have been created for them, the length of the instructional periods will increase. Review and reinforcement activities will also become part of the regular routine. At this point, instructional periods may be as long as thirty to forty minutes, so it is important to vary activities so that students do not become frustrated or bored.

With the portability of the methodology, literacy skill development can extend to other subject areas where students may also engage in learning to read subject words, creating sentences, and reading subject-related worksheets and books. As literacy is the primary component of all learning, when students are fully entrenched in this instructional methodology, literacy skill development will extend across all subjects and become the overall foundation of the academic experience.

Many students who have special learning needs have difficulty sustaining their attention on one activity for long periods of time. To avoid frustration or boredom, it is suggested that teachers include a variety of activities that target specific skill areas.

Consistency of Methodology and Materials

As students move through the grades, they are taught by many different teachers and paraeducators. Often, different teachers use different approaches, resulting in inconsistency that can be disastrous for many students. Most students who have special learning needs, particularly those who are visual learners, need a specialized approach that is based on their strengths. If a particular methodological approach is successful for a student, then it must not be changed because of the personal philosophy of the teacher or paraeducator. For instance, if a student is successful in learning to read through whole word sight recognition, this cannot be abandoned in favor of a completely phonics-based approach.

One way to enable consistency is to provide the student with a bin that contains all of his instructional materials:
- grids and flashcards;
- books that have been created for him;
- print books that he is able to read;
- scrapbooks from previous years;
- review and reinforcement activity materials;
- printing, writing or keyboarding samples;
- math worksheets that clearly show the level at which the student is working;
- articles and books that are relevant;
- outline of the student's habits and preferences;
- outline of previous year's schedule and components of the student's daily participation in literacy activities;
- games and reward activities.

Bins that carry over from one year to the next provide all instructors with valuable information and materials, including the following:
- a visual profile of the student's ability;
- an indication of what skills the student had developed by the end of the previous school year;
- materials for review and reinforcement;
- an automatic supply of materials to be used as the starting point for the new year's program;
- articles and information that address the student's particular profile of learning needs.

The key implication of consistency is that the wheel does not have to be re-invented each year. Regardless of grade change or location (if the student were to move), the teaching staff has a solid foundation of instructional strategies and materials on which to base the student's Individual Education Plans.

> Consistency of instructional approach and continued use of materials that have proven to be helpful for an individual student are key to the student's successful development of academic skills.

Summary:

In preparation for implementing instruction using the Oelwein method, teachers are advised to familiarize themselves with logistics and parameters, such as the materials that will be needed, the optimal environment for teaching, and how to maintain consistency.

Materials that are neatly constructed and visually attractive are engaging and will help to maintain students' interest in literacy-based activities. Keeping instructional materials and work space well-organized will not only help the teacher, but will also help the students develop organizational skills. Students will learn to take care of their flashcards, books, writing materials and games. When students experience success, they will become invested in maintaining the materials that have enabled that success.

CHAPTER FOUR:
ACQUIRING A SIGHT WORD VOCABULARY: IMPLEMENTING THE MATCH, SELECT, AND NAME SEQUENCE

The top down approach of the Oelwein method begins with teaching whole words using the **match, select,** and **name** sequence, taking the student through the four stages of learning as each set of words is taught.

Pre-Skills for Effective Participation in the Program

Pre-requisite skills for being taught literacy skills using the Oelwein method differ considerably from those often required for starting traditional reading programs. Indeed, it is often the readiness requirements of traditional programs that prevent students with learning differences from having the opportunity to learn to read. The pre-skills recommended for undertaking the Oelwein method are table-readiness and matching skills.

Table Readiness

To be considered "table ready," students need to have an awareness of the nature of instructional interaction. Students who are able to sit at a table and respond to and cooperate with the instructor for approximately five minutes at a time are sufficiently qualified.

Many students with Autism Spectrum Disorder have developed table-readiness skills through participation in the direct and intensive instructional sessions of their ABA (Applied Behavioral Analysis) programs in specialized pre-schools or in programs that are delivered at home.

Some children with ASD may initially have difficulty coming to the table, but with the use of personal vocabulary based on their interests, it is usually not difficult to engage them in the process. Often it is best to start with brief periods and gradually work up to longer periods at the worktable.

Matching Skills

> "The ability to match pictures, designs and shapes to identical samples often reveals a number of important abilities. A child who is successful at these tasks is often one who can attend to visual stimuli, discriminate between differing stimuli, and emit specific motor behaviors to complete a task. There are many elements of this skill that are relevant to language training and language development, and important information about a non-verbal child can be obtained by determining the degree to which he can match similar stimuli" (Sundberg & Partington, 1998, p. 24).

Matching is a critical first skill for all learners. The ability to match indicates that children are able to perceive like items in the environment and are beginning to form mental classifications. To begin teaching the matching process, have materials ready that are appropriate for the student. If, for instance, a student is sensitive to louder sounds, use quiet manipulatives, such as pompoms, which can be purchased at craft stores.

A Simple Hierarchy of Matching Skills:
1) **Shape to shape:** Simple shapes, such as circles, squares, and triangles are matched. Many children, particularly some children with ASD, can be distracted by the attributes (texture, sound, color) of objects. It is therefore preferable to start with simple black shapes on a white or pale blue background. Shapes should be cut from tag board (and possibly laminated for durability) and should be approximately 4 inches in size.
2) **Object to object:** Students progress to matching simple objects, such as spoons, attribute blocks, pattern blocks, pencils, erasers, etc. In the beginning, it is important that items be identical so that the teacher can discern that the student has an understanding of sameness.
3) **Picture to picture:** Photographs of simple objects, such as those that were used at the object to object stage, are presented for matching.
4) **Symbol to symbol:** Simple picture symbols, such as those generated by Boardmaker™ (Mayer-Johnson) are matched. If commercial picture symbols are not available, simple drawings can be created to represent toys, foods, locations, etc. to the child. The meaning of the symbols or drawings should be readily apparent to the student.

5) **Object to picture or symbol:** Students match a three-dimensional object to a two-dimensional representation (photograph or picture/picture symbol), indicating they have moved on to the symbolic level.

6) **Picture or symbol to object:** Students understand the abstract representation of an object (picture or symbol) and can match it to the actual object.

Not only do students need to be able to discern sameness, they also need to be able to go through the motor planning process of putting the matching objects on top of or next to one another. Some children may initially need to be physically prompted through this process until the motor planning components of the matching process have been mastered and habituated.

Stage 1: Acquisition

Most students who have the necessary prerequisite skills of being ready to sit at the table and being able to match are able to learn four words during the first session. In fact, many students are able to learn eight words and participate in making simple sentences immediately. When students demonstrate mastery of whole word sight recognition, it is critical to move forward, adding new words as soon as previously taught words are embedded.

Students for whom initially introducing four words may be too challenging can be taken through a simpler process, as outlined below. The steps are clearly described and provide the instructional model for working with students at all levels, from those at the most basic level to those who are able to make more rapid progress in the acquisition stage.

Determine initial vocabulary

Initial vocabulary words must be **high interest**, meaningful words such as the names of family members, friends, or special interests. Include the words *I* and *see* or *like* among the first eight words taught so that students can begin working on sentence construction as soon as possible.

The Process:

Note: Many students are able to begin with a four-word grid.

• **Introduce the first word**

  o **Match 1:1:** Abby will match the flashcard to the matching word on the picture card (a picture of herself).

    ▸ Place the student's picture card in front of her. The card will have a picture of the student with her name written below it.

    ▸ Point to the picture and say, "It's Abby. Point to Abby." (If "Abby" is not in her speaking vocabulary, pair the hand sign for Abby with the word each time you say it.)

    ▸ Point to the word *Abby* on the picture card and say, "This says, *Abby.*"

‣Give her the matching flashcard (the word *Abby*) and say, "This says *Abby*. Put the word *Abby* on *Abby*." (You may need to demonstrate this and/or gently guide her hand to place the *Abby* flashcard on the word *Abby* on the picture card.)

‣Repeat until she places the flashcard on the matching word unassisted.

‣ Provide feedback for each response.

• **Select 1:2:** Abby will select the *Abby* flashcard from a choice of two flashcards, the *Abby* flashcard and a blank flashcard.

o Leave the picture card on the table in front of the student.

o Show her two flashcards (the *Abby* flashcard and the blank one), and say, "Pick up *Abby*."

o When she takes it say, "Put *Abby* on *Abby*" (pointing to the name on the picture card).

o Repeat until she selects and matches the *Abby* flashcard with the word *Abby* on the picture card.

o Provide feedback for each response.

• **Name:** Abby will read her name on the flashcard.

o With the picture card on the table, show Abby the *Abby* flashcard and say, "This word says ____." Wait for her to say or sign her name.

o If she does not say or sign it, cue her by pointing to the picture; if she does not respond, tell her, "It says, *Abby*."

o Give her the flashcard and tell her to put *Abby* (flashcard) on the word *Abby* (picture card).

o Provide feedback for each response.

• **Introduce a second word**

o Follow same procedures as for introducing the first word: match (1:1), select (1:2), and name the word *Mom*, except when selecting, use the *Abby* flashcard as the second flashcard, rather than a blank one.

• **Discriminate between two words**

o **Match 1:2:** Abby will match with two choices:

‣ Place both picture cards (Abby and Mom) in front of Abby.

‣ Point to the pictures, saying, *"Abby"* and *"Mom"* (or let her supply the names if she is able and willing).

‣ Give her the matching flashcards, one at a time, saying, "*Abby*. Put the word *Abby* on *Abby*," and, "*Mom*. Put the word *Mom* on *Mom*" (word on flashcard to word on picture card).

‣ Provide feedback.

- **Select 1:2:** Abby will select with two choices (one word, two choices):
  - ▸ Leave the picture cards on the table in front of the child.
  - ▸ Hold up the two flashcards (*Abby* and *Mom*) and say, "Take the word *Mom*."
  - ▸ She takes *Mom* and matches it with the Mom picture card.
  - ▸ Hold up the two flashcards again and say, "Take *Abby*."
  - ▸ She takes the *Abby* flashcard and matches it with the Abby picture card.
  - ▸ Leave the picture cards on the table, and place the flashcards beside them. Ask the child to point to each word as you say it.
  - ▸ If she makes a mistake, show her how she can look the word up using the picture card. She just needs to match the word and look at the picture as the picture defines the word.
  - ▸ Remove the picture cards and ask her to point to each word.
  - ▸ Provide feedback if she recognizes words without looking them up.

- **Name:** Abby will read the flashcards either verbally or using hand signs.
  - Leave the picture cards on the table.
  - Present each flashcard, one at a time, saying, "This says …."
  - As she reads each flashcard (verbally or by sign), she matches it with the word on the picture card.
  - If she makes a mistake, show her how she can look up the word on the picture card.
  - Remove the picture cards and ask her to read each flashcard.
  - Provide feedback; she just read her first two words!

- **Introduce additional words**
  - Introduce additional names and words that can be illustrated using the same method described above, increasing the choices as new words are introduced.

Word Grids				
#1	**#2**	**#3**	**#4**	**#5**
4 names of persons (or pets) who are important to the child	*I* *see* + 2 more names	*like* *and* + 2 names of persons or things that the child likes	4 words derived from items or characters the child likes	*the* *go* *school* *bus*

○ Continue to add vocabulary words that will facilitate sentence building such as *here*, *is*, *my*, *to* (words common to primer word lists). When presenting four-word grids, pair two sentence builders with two nouns, verbs or adjectives.

○ Make sentences using the flashcards and have the student read them.
  ‣ *I see Abby.*
  ‣ *I see Mom.*
  ‣ *I see Dad.*
  ‣ *I see Sissy.*

• **Create a personal dictionary**
  ○ As the student's vocabulary grows, she can record her vocabulary words in a personal dictionary (a regular school notebook with one letter per page). This dictionary can be used as a tool for review and spelling reference.

• **Label objects in the environment**
  ○ The names of objects in the environment can be taught by labeling objects:
    ‣ Make two sets of flashcards for each object, such as *door, window, table, chair*.
    ‣ Use one set of flashcards as labels, taping the labels to the objects within easy reach of the child.
    ‣ Label up to four objects at time.
    ‣ The student completes the match, select, and name sequence with each word, matching the flashcards to the labels on the actual objects, rather than the word on a picture card.
    ‣ Proceed through the stages of learning with these words.
    ‣ Chairs, desks, and cubbies should be labeled with students' names.

• **Create the student's first book**

Abby's Book

I like Daddy.

o Use card stock to make a cover. Title the book, *Abby's Book.*
  ▸ Teach her the word *book* by having her match the *book* flashcard with the word *book* in the title (she selects from *Abby* and *book).*
  ▸ Glue a picture of a person or pet onto each page. Under the picture, carefully print, "*I see X* (name of person or pet)."
  ▸ Abby reads her book (either verbally or by hand sign) with pleasure and pride.

- **Use a probe to evaluate**
  o At the end of each teaching session, remove the picture cards. Ask the student to read the flashcards as you "flash" them, giving her ample time to ponder each card.
  o Place the cards she reads correctly under a happy face drawn on a large card, saying, "Right!"
  o Place the cards she reads incorrectly, or to which she gives no response, under a neutral face drawn on a card (mouth straight across, not sad or happy), saying, "Try again."

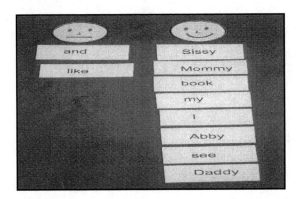

- **Prepare a simple graph for recording reading progress (See Appendix T4.1. for reproducible template)**
  o Have the student point to the words she read correctly, and those she missed (the ones she needs to practice). Did she get more right than wrong? If she missed more than she got right, determine why and re-teach. The student may not be ready to read and it may be necessary to put off instruction, or words may need to be introduced more slowly.
  o Count the number of words she read correctly and mark this number on the Reading Progress Graph.
  o Have the student participate in making the graph, coloring it and marking the number of correct responses.

- **Add a word and drop a word**
  o Continue the probe with all the words that have been introduced, until the student has ten words in her reading vocabulary. After that, keep just ten words in the

probe, dropping words that have been mastered, and adding new words as they are introduced.

- **Start a word bank**
  - When words are dropped from the probe, put these flashcards in the student's word bank. These words are stored for future uses including:
    - ▶ Arranging them to compose sentences;
    - ▶ Filing them when the alphabet is introduced;
    - ▶ Looking up the spelling of a word;
    - ▶ Keeping a record of words mastered, fostering the child's pride in her "bank account."

Stage 2: Fluency
Review and Reinforcement
Now that the child has learned to read words, review and practice are essential for developing fluency. It is important to use fun and engaging activities for review and practice. Students must have a reason to match, select, and name the words, and playing games provides a good reason. Games and activities provide opportunities for review and reinforcement. Having students play games with peers is an excellent inclusion activity.

Stage 3: Transfer
Reading Words with Different Presentations
At this stage, students are taught to recognize the word, regardless of the way it is presented, including in different fonts, with different size letters, on different colors of paper, and different colors of print. Students participate in activities designed to teach them to recognize the word regardless of the way it is presented. The computer is a very useful tool at this stage as it allows for virtually instant preparation of materials in different font styles, sizes, and colors.

- **Sample Activities**:
  - Students match like words printed in different fonts, letter sizes, and printed on different-colored paper.
  - Students use stick-on labels with names on them to mark ownership of books, magazines, tapes, CDs, DVDs and toys, as well as to state "to" and "from" on art projects and gifts.
  - Students put place cards on the table where family members sit.
  - Students find their papers and other belongings marked with their name.
  - Students read simple sentences and books prepared in different fonts and colors.
  - Students read commercially available print books at their reading level, and related to their interests, such as a favorite story/cartoon characters.

Stage 4: Generalization
Reading Words Anywhere, Anytime

Many students, particularly those with ASD, are not able to recognize their vocabulary words with 100% consistency from one day to the next due to a variety of performance difficulties, particularly in the area of word retrieval. It may be assumed that students with a response consistency rate of 75% or more recognize the words, but may not be able to express that recognition with regularity. For students with ASD, selection may be far more accurate than naming. Once words are consistently recognized in the generalization stage, they are embedded in long-term memory and recognized in any format, in any context. Reviewing these words is seldom necessary.

Breaks and Burn-out

Occasionally, students become tired of their work and turn off; this may be referred to as a "plateau." This is generally not something to worry about. Look at it as a period of consolidation: the child needs time to assimilate what she has learned and needs a break before moving on. Acknowledge the situation and change activities. For one child, this may mean leaving her reading program for a couple of weeks. For another, it may mean putting aside mathematics. When a child consistently does not want to engage and appears to have reached a wall, focus on another domain, such as fine or gross motor skill development, or the development of listening skills through story-reading or videos. After an adequate break, return to reading, but with a new theme or activity. The child's behavior and degree of engagement will make clear when she is ready to resume reading instruction.

Sight Word Recognition: Review and Reinforcement Activities
Sample activities for review/practice
Lotto Games:

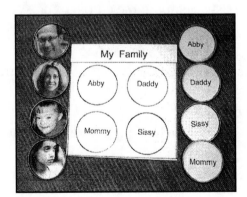

- Games consist of a **game board** with four to eight words and **game pieces** (cards or disks) to match to the words on the game board.

- **Title each lotto game board** according to the category of the words on it.
  - The first lotto game may be titled *My Family*.
  - A second lotto game that includes the words, *I, see,* and *book* may be titled, *My Words*.
  - Additional lotto games titled according to unit or category may include:
    - *All about Me* (body parts);
    - *What I Do* (action words: *play, read, jump, run, swing, swim,* etc.);
    - *How I Feel* (feeling words: *happy, sad, angry, cold, hot, sick,* etc.);
    - Color words;
    - Animal words.

- **Content on matching game pieces** can consist of:
  - The same words that are on the game board, in the same or different font;
  - A picture or symbol (line drawing or hand sign for the word) to match with the word to practice comprehension (matching the "definition" with the word):
    - photos of family members to match with the name;
    - line drawings or photo of child with arrows pointing to the body part to match with the name of the body part;
    - line drawings or photos that demonstrate actions to match with the action words;
    - line drawings of faces demonstrating feelings to match with feeling words;
    - colors to match with the name of the color;
    - pictures of animals to match with the name of the animal.

Making lotto games:
- **Game board:** use card stock or similar material and proceed as follows:
  - Print the title at the top of the game board.
  - Divide the rest of the board into the same number of spaces as there are words in the game (rectangles spaces for game cards; circles for game disks).
  - Print the words in the spaces and laminate, if necessary.
  - Make three copies of the game board—one to be the actual game board, one to cut up for the game cards, and one to cut for a concentration game.

- **Game cards and/or disks:**
  - **rectangular game cards:** can be made by copying and cutting the game board into sections
  - **matching word cards:** cut to fit in the spaces on the game card (laminate if necessary)
  - **picture game cards:** to match with the word on the game board, glue the photo (or line drawing) on card stock, cut to fit rectangles on game board, and laminate.
  - **game disks:** add variety and give a game-like quality
  - **matching word disk:** draw or copy (See Appendix T4.2. & T4.3. for circle templates) circles onto card stock that are sized to fit inside can or bottle caps to

make game disks [use frozen concentrate juice can lids for larger disks (2 ½ inches, 6 ½ cm); gallon-size bottle caps (1 ½ inches; 3 ½ cm) for smaller disks], print in the word, laminate, glue in juice can lids, or insert in the grooves of bottle caps.

   o **picture disks:** glue the picture on cardstock, draw a circle the size of the lid or cap around the picture, laminate, cut it out and glue on the can lid or fit in the grooves of the bottle caps.

Play lotto:

- Turn the game cards (or disks) face down, mix them up (children enjoy mixing).
- Select a card (or disk).
- Read the word or name the picture.
- Match the card/disk to the word on the game board (picture to word demonstrates comprehension).
- Continue until the card is filled.
- Student scores for each correct match.

*To give students an opportunity to move around, hide game cards (or disks) and have students hunt for them; as they find each card (or disk), they read it (found *Dad*) and match it on the game board.

Concentration:

This game consists of a **game board** and **two sets of game cards** or disks.

- **Game board:** a grid made of cardstock and laminated
   o Start with a grid composed of four spaces the size of the game card or disk.
   o Move to a six-space grid when the student is successful playing on four-spaces grid and has six words in the practice stage.
   o Increase the number of spaces on the game board to up to 12 spaces; be sure and keep the number at the child's success level—change the game cards as he learns new words, but don't make the game too difficult for him.

- **Game cards and disks** are the same as those for lotto, except there are two of each word card or word disk.

- **Play concentration:** This game is better using disks—they make it game-like and they are easy for students to pick up from the board—all the disks for a game should be the same color).

- **Word to Word Concentration.** Create a game board with twice as many spaces as you have words (i.e., four words = eight spaces), and have two word disks for each word.

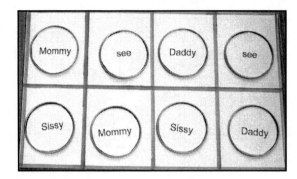

- Turn disks face down; mix them up (children enjoy doing this).
- Place a disk in each space on the grid, face down.
- Player turns a disk over, then turns a second one over:
- If it is a match, he has won both disks and takes them off the board;
- If there is no match, and his is playing alone, he turns them both over and tries again;
- If there is another player, he turns them over and she takes her turn.
- The game is over when the board is cleared; if there are two players, the one that has more disks wins.

- **Word to Picture Concentration.** Play concentration as outlined above, with word disks and matching pictures disks; players will be looking for a picture match with the word, or a word match with the picture, whichever one he turns over first.

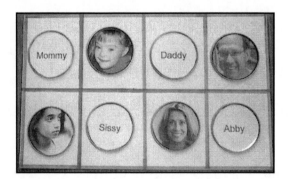

The Fishing Game:
- Put metal paper clips or a magnetic strip on flashcards and place them in a "pond."
- Make a fishing pole for each player by stringing a magnet to the end of a stick/pencil.
- Students "fish" for words and read the words they "catch."
- Game can be extended by having students sort their words by category or by the first letter of the word.

• This is a great game for taking turns and involving peers—everyone likes The Fishing Game!

Bingo:
• Make Bingo cards consisting of nine spaces with a word printed in each space; each card should have a different arrangement of words and should have words all the players can read.
• The "caller" draws a flashcard and reads it.
• Players scan their cards for the word read by the caller and place a token on the word if they have it.
• Three tokens in a row, vertical, horizontal, or diagonal, wins the game—Bingo!

Word Rings:
• Rings can generally be purchased in a package in the binder section of most stationary stores.
• Punch a hole in the upper left corner of each flashcard.
• Thread the flashcards on the word ring.
• The student flips the cards on the ring and reads them.
• As the student collects these word rings, he can make choices about reviewing. Hold up two or three word rings and ask the student which one he would like to go through (this removes the issue of compliance and gives the student some autonomy over the process).
• Conversely, the teacher and student take turns reading the words on the ring, with the teacher making occasional deliberate errors to see if the student will detect them.
• Word rings can also be used as a means of communication for non-verbal students: students find the words for the messages they want to communicate and show them to their teacher or partner (example: *break, toilet, water, thank you, please, hello,* etc.).

Treasure Hunt:
• Play "treasure hunt" using the names of objects in the environment.
• Number envelopes and enclose clues in the order of the hunt,:
    ○ 1 - the first clue, *teacher's desk,* is enclosed
    ○ 2 - the second clue, *Emma's desk,* is enclosed
    ○ 3 - the third clue, *John's cubby,* is enclosed
    ○ 4 - the fourth card, names the "treasure" or treat the student wins
• The player opens the first clue, reads *teacher's desk,* and looks for the second clue that is taped to or hidden on the teacher's desk.
• The player finds the second clue, opens it, and reads *Emma's desk,* and goes to Emma's desk to find the third clue, *John's cubby.*
• The player goes to John's cubby and finds the fourth card, opens it, and reads what that the treasure is, or the actual treasure can be located inside the cubby.

• Treasure hunt can be played at home with clues such as *Mom's dresser, Dad's chair, Jason's bed*, etc.

Summary:

As students continually engage in the four stages of learning, they will expand reading, spoken, and written vocabulary. It's important that students not be held up at the acquisition stage after words have been learned. Keep the process moving so that students do not become bored and disenchanted with the process.

Participation in a variety of review and reinforcement activities should be a daily part of literacy instruction. These activities can also be done at home, aiding in the process of skill transfer to other environments. Once students have built a sight word vocabulary, learning to use their words in the broader context of literacy will be the next challenge.

<u>Tip Sheet</u>

Stages of Learning: the Oelwein Approach

1) Acquisition — The Foundation of the Methodology

  Level 1: Matching. Matching is the simplest response. The student matches the word on a flashcard to a matching picture of that same word on a picture card.

• Using the word grid and flashcards, tell the child what each word is and ask him to put _____ (flashcard) on top of _____ (corresponding picture card). Tell him that he is <u>matching.</u>

• Ask the student to match each word.

• Repeat the entire process two more times.

  Level 2: Selecting. The student selects the correct word flashcard on verbal and/or signed cue.

• Lay the four flashcards on the desk in random order.

• Ask the student to pick up a certain word and give it to you (gesture to the palm of your hand).

• If the child has difficulty, guide his hand to find it.

• Tell the student to close his eyes while you mix up the cards and repeat the selection process two more times (3 times total).

  Level 3: Naming. Naming (saying or signing the word) in response to the written word, is the most complex response.

• If a verbal student is confident and ready, show him the word flashcard and ask him to name word on the card.

• If the student is non-verbal, teach hand signs for vocabulary words.

• Some students with ASD prefer to select the flashcards as it given them autonomy over the process and can help reduce retrieval anxiety. For these students, put the flashcards on the table and ask them to give the cards to you, naming them in whatever order they wish.

IMPORTANT: For students who are non-verbal, <u>selecting</u> the correct word at your request indicates <u>recognition</u> of the word. Placing the flashcard on the correct picture indicates an understanding of what the word means. To test for <u>comprehension,</u> ask students to match words to pictures or objects.

2) Fluency: The student has learned to read the word, but now needs practice and regular review to become fluent. Practice by playing matching and naming games, such as lotto and bingo. Record the student's words and chart the rate of recognition.

3) Transfer: The student is able to read words represented in different fonts, on different colors of paper and with different size letters.

4) Generalization: The student has learned to read the word in any print form or medium.

<u>Vocabulary Development</u>

• Add new words to the student's sight vocabulary on an ongoing basis.

• Maintain the student's interest and enthusiasm through the use of personal and meaningful vocabulary.

• Record the student's words in a personal dictionary.

<u>Sentence Construction:</u>

• Each literacy period should have a sentence building component.

• Initially, sentences can be constructed with flashcards.

• The student will work towards using a keyboard to input sentences into a word processing program or printing them in a notebook (if printing is a viable or realistic option).

5

CHAPTER FIVE:
SIGN-ASSISTED LITERACY

At the National Down Syndrome Conference in 1997, I attended a workshop on language development. During the workshop, my attention was piqued by a parent who talked about the effect that learning sign language had had on her son's ability to speak. He was an older boy who had never been able to articulate clearly enough to be understood and had thus experienced a great deal of frustration in trying to communicate with others. The mother had refused to have him taught sign language as a child because she had been afraid that he would not learn to talk if he had another, easier way to communicate.

Finally, when intelligible speech no longer appeared to be a possibility, she allowed him to learn sign language. As a result, his verbal speech slowly, but surely, began to develop. She pleaded with other parents in the audience to be open to the use of sign language if their children were unable to speak or articulate well enough to make themselves understood.

I was both touched and inspired by this woman's story and resolved to explore this issue further as I had several students (some with ASD, some with DS) who had significant difficulty with articulation or who were non-verbal. I could recall instances when these students had used gestures to communicate. Having used the Oelwein approach with them, I knew that these students were able to identify words: they were able to match and select them and place flashcards on the appropriate pictures. The only missing piece was the naming process and it seemed a logical step to introduce sign language as their mode of expression.

— L. Broun

In his book, *Next of Kin* (1997), Roger Fouts discusses his experience of using sign language with his students with autism to facilitate speech. He set out to understand why signing promotes speech. He found his answer in the work of Dr. Doreen Kimura of the University of Western Ontario.

"Kimura explained to me that the region of the brain that controlled speech also appeared to control precise hand movements...Sign language uses gesture of the hands; spoken language is gesture of the tongue. The tongue makes precise movements, stopping at specific places around the mouth so that we can produce certain sounds. The hands and fingers stop at precise places around the body to produce signs. These precision movements of the tongue and hands are not just related, they are connected through the motor regions of the brain. Darwin noted this connection...when people move their fingers very precisely—while threading a needle, for example, they often make sympathetic movements with their tongues" (Fouts, 1997, p. 190-191).

Fouts noted that Kimura had observed that people make certain kinds of free hand movements only when they are moving their tongues when speaking. Through her research, she confirmed the existence of a bridge in the neural mechanism that connects the movements of the hands with movements of the tongue. This information reinforced the efficacy of combining the printed word with hand signs. Not only does signing allow non-verbal students to express their ability to read, it may also expand their communication skills.

Fouts was impressed by the results of implementing the use of hand signs with his students. One student, a young man with Down syndrome, gained a sight and sign vocabulary of over one thousand words. His vocal attempts became more and more accurate. He was more confident and less frustrated as others were able to understand his communicative attempts and perceive him as a learner. Likewise, many other students who were non-verbal or who had struggled with articulation were also able to express their recognition of words and participate in the reading process through the use of hand signs.

For some children, hand signs act as visual cues that prompt vocalization.

"A child can use signs to prompt his own vocalizations. That is, if non-verbal stimuli can evoke a sign and the child is able to emit a vocalization under the control of a sign, then he can self-prompt his own vocalizations... This self-prompting may result in more successful vocal-verbal interactions and more reinforcements for attempts to speak" (Sundberg, M. & Partington, J.,1998, p. 78).

Sundberg & Partington (1998) also point out that learning sign language may be easier for special needs students than learning to speak, "because many non-verbal children cannot echo sounds or words, but they can imitate at least some of the fine or gross motor movements of others...however, it should be pointed out that a strong imitative repertoire is not a prerequisite for the use of signs" (Sundberg & Partington, 1998, p. 74).

When the printed word is paired with a hand sign, reading the word may also become a prompt for speech. When students are learning new words with hand signs, they experience the following pathways for learning:
- Visual: they see both the printed word and the motions of the hand sign;
- Auditory: they hear the word spoken;
- Kinesthetic: they go through the physical process of learning to construct the sign; they make and use the sign in order to communicate via a gestural, rather than verbal, response.

This parallels the experience of verbal students participating in the reading process, the only difference being that non-verbal students use their hands rather than their mouths. Sign-assisted literacy cannot be ignored as a tool for developing both literacy and communication skills, as one will certainly affect the other.

Some useful guidelines for the implementation of sign-assisted literacy
1) Obtain parent permission for using sign language. Supportive families reinforce the student's communicative attempts and reading at home.
2) As the student learns new sight words and their signs, send the sign diagrams home for the family.
3) Teach the signs to other willing classmates and friends.
4) Be flexible around sign formation. If the student cannot form the sign exactly, improvise with an adaptive sign (the formation of a hand sign that may be individual to the child and will be understood by his family and school support team).
5) Do not be intimidated by the use of sign. There is no need to take a course or to become a fluent signer. Learn the signs one at a time, just like the student.
*Note: If a student is able to make verbal responses at any point in the process of learning to express word recognition with hand signs, encourage verbal response; when/if verbal response becomes consistent, discontinue use of the sign.

Implementing the Oelwein Method Using Sign-Assisted Literacy

The Acquisition Process
1) Pair the sign diagram with the printed word (or put the sign diagram on the back of a flashcard). Sign diagrams can be minimized on the copier in order to fit on the flashcard.

2) When demonstrating how to form a hand sign, sit beside the student, not across from him. This will allow the student to parallel your movements rather than having to process the visual reversals.
3) Pair the sign with the spoken word while teaching the student to match.
4) Implement the match, select, and name process, substituting the expectation of the hand sign for the spoken word as the student's mode of expression.
5) If the child is able to say the word, discontinue use of the sign.

Practice to Fluency Using Hand Sign
- The student can participate in all of the review and reinforcement activities used with verbal students, substituting signed responses for verbal responses.
- In the case of the non-verbal student, both word recognition and sign formation are being reinforced, thus the development of fluency may be somewhat slower.
- Because the non-verbal student is participating in the dual task of word recognition and sign formation, it is important to be attentive to:
  ○ How quickly the student is acquiring signs,
  ○ The ease with which he makes the signs,
  ○ Providing a great deal of positive reinforcement for his participation in the process,
  ○ Continued modeling of signs as necessary. (In some instances, the student may need a visual or physical prompt; however, it is important to fade prompts as quickly as possible.)
- When the student is able to recognize the word and make the hand sign at a high rate of fluency, remove the sign diagram from the flashcard. Do not retain it as a visual cue any longer than necessary.

Transfer
For students who use hand signs to express word recognition, the transfer process is two-fold:
1) Just as for the verbal student, the non-verbal student must demonstrate the ability to indicate word recognition when words are presented in different fonts, formats, etc.
2) Because the student is engaging in a personal, physical act (forming the hand signs), he will need to practice reading in various settings so that he is able to use his hand signs to read across environments. While it is also important for the verbal student to engage in reading across environments, the student who signs must learn to transfer the physical as well as the cognitive component.

Generalization
- The student has embedded recognition of the word in long-term memory and is able to recognize it consistently.
- The student is able to make the hand sign for the word consistently in all environments.

Summary:

Sign is a symbolic means of expressing thought, just as spoken words are also symbols. Sign-assisted literacy allows both non-verbal students and students with emergent verbal skills to participate in reading, an activity from which they might otherwise have been excluded because of the erroneous assumption that speech is necessary for engagement in reading. Very often, the signs that the student learns through reading transfer to the communication process, so while the non-verbal student's task is two fold (word and sign), the benefits of learning to read using hand signs are also two fold.

PART II

WE HAVE WORDS!

NOW WHAT DO WE DO WITH THEM?

CHAPTER SIX:
GRAMMAR AND SENTENCE CONSTRUCTION

At a workshop several years ago, a parent approached me at the break to tell me about her son, a five-year-old boy with autism who was non-verbal. She had been working with him on the match, select, and name method for several weeks and he had acquired a sizeable number of words that he could recognize. His flashcards were stored in a zipped sandwich bag.

One Saturday morning as he and his father were watching cartoons, the boy dropped his bag of flashcards and they spilled on to the floor. As he was picking them up, he put the following words together: *I see Mommy.* Then, he pointed to the ceiling. Indeed, Mommy was upstairs in the shower. This was his first communication with language. — L. Broun

One of the cornerstones of the Oelwein method is the selection of vocabulary words that are immediately useful to the learner. It is critical to show students that words have a purpose and can be manipulated to have meaning, perhaps the most essential component in the development of literacy skills. As students progress, sentence builders, such as the words on Dolch word list, are also included. In fact, for most students, the words *I* and *see* may be included in their second grid, allowing for the construction of six sentences. Further adding the word, *like*, allows for twelve sentences.

I see Mommy.	*I like Mommy.*
I see Daddy.	*I like Daddy.*
I see Susie.	*I like Susie.*
I see Fluffy.	*I like Fluffy.*
I see Grandma.	*I like Grandma.*
I see Mrs. Smith.	*I like Mrs. Smith.*

Ongoing practice in sentence construction is one of the most critical and useful activities for helping students develop competency in understanding and using language. Practice in sentence construction should be a component of daily instruction in literacy skill development. With ongoing practice, students will become habituated to the format of sentences. This habituation is critical. Eventually, students will be able to formulate sentences independently using flashcards, indicating that:
- The format of a sentence has been embedded,
- The printed word is understood to convey meaning,
- The meaning of a particular group of words is understood.

Rote memorization of sentence structure may give students a framework within which to express coherent thoughts and give responses (in spoken or gestural language) in a grammatically structured manner. Using a student's reading vocabulary for sentence construction helps enable the student to develop an understanding of the structure and patterns of both spoken and written language. With ongoing practice in both constructing and reading sentences, the student may be more receptive to the communication of others. Not having to struggle with understanding the construction of spoken language may facilitate comprehension of spoken messages. Through print, it is possible to provide a visual means by which to assist students with organizing their internal language for thought, thereby contributing to the development of thinking, communication, and academic skills.

> Grammar provides the framework for thought.

The Sentence Board

As previously stated, it is usually possible to begin sentence reading and sentence building activities very early in the learning process, starting with only a few words. The sentence board is a simple tool that can be used to start the process.

Materials required for creating a sentence board include foam board or sturdy tag board, tape, and two half-inch strips of black tag board (to create two lips for holding the flashcards).

Steps for Creating a Sentence Board:

1) Create a duplicate set of the student's flashcards.

> **Important:** All flashcards should be made from white tag board or card stock so that the visual image the student receives is a unified visual picture. The object is for the student to see the sentence as a unit; a choppy grouping of different colors of paper may distract the student from the goal of creating and reading a coherent grouping of words.

2) Using the student's words, create a short sentence on the top row: *I see Daddy*.

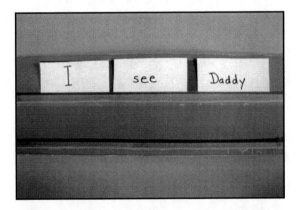

3) Demonstrate the expectation of replicating the sentence in the bottom lip of tag board. You may have to do this several times to ensure the expectation is understood.

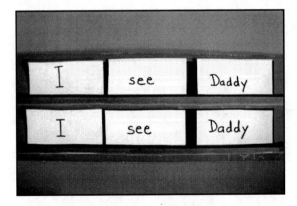

4) Give the student the appropriate flashcards to recreate the sentence and ask him to reproduce the sentence on the bottom row.

5) Ask the student to read the sentence.

6) If he makes an error, ask the student to reread and say, "let's fix it," or just, "fix." Don't go into a lengthy explanation of why there was an error; at this point, it is crucial to keep instructional language to a minimum. Sometimes, it may be necessary to make the correction and point it out to the child: show him that it is now the same as the first sentence, and have him re-read it.

7) Very early in the process, it may be possible for the student to create sentences independently. After a period of practice, he can be given a group of words and be instructed to "make a sentence." It may take some experimentation, but the student is learning that he can manipulate these words to make meaning.

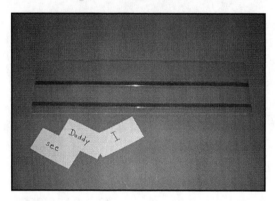

8) Use the student's vocabulary words in as many combinations as possible to create sentences. As the student's vocabulary increases, the length and complexity of the sentences should also increase.

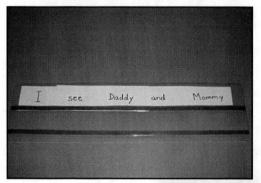 

9) Each instructional session should include the component of asking the student to create sentences independently using a pre-set grouping of flashcards. This will enable the teacher to monitor the student's growing competency in organizing language.

10) When the student has demonstrated a reasonably consistent competency in sentence construction, ask him to create sentences from his bank of word cards, rather than from a pre-set grouping.

11) The objective of this exercise is for the student to be able to create sentences on the sentence board and then either copy them into a notebook or input them into a word processing program on the computer. The student can take the sentence board to the computer and type it. This can be saved and a collection of sentences can be accumulated in the student's paper file or computer documents file.

12) In the final stage, the student is able to bypass the sentence board, create his own sentences, and type or write them directly into a book or computer file. Not all students will reach this stage of independence, but they will reach one of the stages along the way.

Sentence Board Variations: Novelty

• **Cookie sheet:** small strips of magnet tape are applied to the flashcards and sentences are constructed on the cookie sheet.

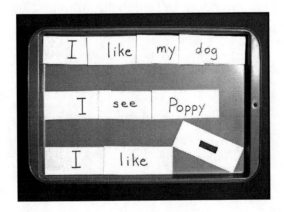

• **Magnetized Board:** Black or green boards are sometimes magnetized, making it possible to use the flashcards to create sentences on those surfaces as well. An advantage to using the black/green board is that the child can print with chalk underneath the sentence.

• **Black and White Board:** This sentence board is created with a piece of black tag board. The white lines are made by rolling typing correction tape along the surface. Clear tape is then placed over the white lines so that they do not deteriorate.

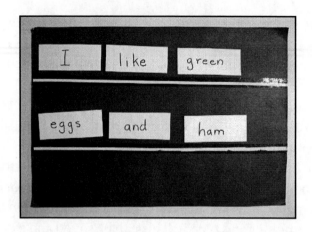

Summary:

Ongoing daily practice of sentence construction is perhaps the most useful skill-building activity in which a student can participate, as it compels the student to work on the internal organization of words to form ideas and thoughts. Initially, the student replicates sentences with flashcards and then works towards independent sentence construction using a word processing program on the computer, or by handwriting. This daily practice habituates sentence structure: it gives the student a rote memory for sentence structure and provides a framework for both delivering and receiving language. As the student becomes more familiar with grammar and syntax through reading, he is better able to apply his visual memory for vocabulary and sentence structure to communication, both for social interaction and for sharing and receiving academic information.

7

CHAPTER SEVEN:
BOOKS

"We are only literate in material for which we have some frame of reference, some level of experience. To understand words, we must understand the world in which the words are being used. This is fundamental to the ability to read" (Goodman, 1995, p. 24).

One of the most pleasurable aspects of teaching literacy skills is watching a child graduate into the world of books. Many students with special learning needs have had extensive experience with having stories read to them by their parents or other caregivers and are comfortable with listening to stories, while others are new to this situation and are participating in literacy-based activities for the first time. Regardless of background, once students have six to eight words in their vocabularies they are sufficiently prepared for actively participating in the process of reading books. At this stage, reading will take on a new format—the students will be the readers and the teachers or caregivers, the listeners.

Books Created Specifically for the Child

The best way to introduce a child to books is to create a book or books specifically for that child that focuses on his family members, individual interests, and life at school and in the community. The individualized book is personally relevant to the student and the "story" is not abstract—the student knows the characters and the settings. The world of print now has real meaning, and the student with special learning needs is invested in the process of reading.

As students learn to read books, they experience a great deal of positive reinforcement and a boost in self-confidence. They come to perceive themselves as members of the literate community and are perceived as such by others. The act of reading has only positive associations, and the "work" proves to be worth it—each new word learned, each new story read, is a great accomplishment that builds pride and self-esteem.

Perhaps most importantly, learning to read and developing an appreciation of books provides students with a life-long source of pleasure. Favorite books may be read over and over again and, as students mature and develop new interests, new books can be added to their personal collection. Reading books is not simply an academic exercise, it is way of enhancing students' lives.

> Jason has Down syndrome. His mother was concerned about his behavior—he was obsessed with trash. She could not keep him out of it. He was constantly exploring the contents of every trashcan, and he was fascinated with the magnificent trucks that came to pick up the trash.
>
> Rather than forbidding him from having anything to do with trash, it was recommended to his mother that she embrace his interest and help him to learn and talk about trash. She made a book, *All about Trash,* so that he could, indeed, become an expert on the subject. The book described what trash was, the men and truck that came for it, and the importance of leaving it in the trashcans. Jason and his mother photographed trashcans at home and in the community and put the pictures in his book. One page was devoted to the reasons why trashcans were off limits.
>
> Jason had his own trashcan stocked with items he and his mother put in it each day: objects and pictures that provided useful vocabulary. He could explore his trashcan whenever he liked. Jason would remove and display the items in his trashcan, name them, and then his mother would write them down for his "trash journal." His trash journal became a checklist of all the things that he had found in his trashcan. Each day, Jason found new items in his trashcan, named what he found, and his mother added the new items to the list. His obsession was no longer a problem, as it had become Jason's "area of expertise." He and his mother could talk and read about trash, building vocabulary and sentence structure in the process. When he started obsessing, his mother would say, "We can't talk about that now. You have to wait until it is time to talk and read about trash."
>
> — P. Oelwein

Starter Books

The Autobiography

A student's first book is usually an *I See* or *I Like* book. Unless the child has demonstrated a special interest, a good choice for a second book is often an autobiography, or *All About Me* book. Autobiographies can build children's self image and provide them with vocabulary and sentence structure to talk about themselves and answer social questions. The autobiography should be an ongoing work-in-progress, with new information added on a regular basis.

The following is sample content for an autobiography, consisting of one sentence per page:
- *My name is Emma.*
- *I am a girl* (picture or drawing of the girl, perhaps in a dress).
- *I am five years old* (birthday pictures or drawing of birthday cake with candles).
- *My eyes are blue* (picture or drawing that shows the color of her eyes).
- *My hair is long* (picture or drawing).
- *My hand is this big* (trace hand).
- *My foot is this big* (trace foot).
- *I like Barbie dolls* (picture of her holding dolls).

To teach body parts, the following pages may be included:
- *I have two eyes/ two ears/ one nose/ one mouth.*
- *My neck/ chest/ tummy/ arms/ legs/ hands/ feet.*

The "My Family" Book
Pages for a *My Family* book may read:
- *This is my Mommy.*
- *Here is my Daddy.*
- *Here is my brother, Josh. He is a baby.*
- *Here is my grandma.*
- *Here is my grandpa.*
- *This is my cat, Mick.*
- *This is my house. We all live here.*

The "My School" Book
Sample content includes:
- *My name is Emma Jones.*
- *I am six years old.*
- *I go to Edison Elementary School.*
- *I am in grade one.*
- *My teacher is Ms Clarke.*
- *These are my friends.*
- *This is my friend, Greg.*

More advanced biographies might contain first and last names of family members, the student's address, phone number, doctors and dentist names and their phone numbers, in order to help the student access and recall personal information.

Personal Experience Books

To create a personal experience book, inquire about experiences and activities that interest the student. Take photos and ask parents for photographs of experiences and outings the student enjoyed. Create these personal books with simple sentences that the student can use when telling others about his experiences.

> One of my students was very interested in furnaces. Whenever he walked into a building or home, he wanted to know where the furnace was. This was a good topic of conversation and a subject that could easily be expanded on through reading. His personal book had pictures of furnaces: his furnace, Grandma and Grandpa's furnace, the school furnace, church furnace, a gas furnace, oil furnace, electric heat with no furnace, thermostats that tell the furnace when to come on and go off, registers where the heat comes out— there is no end to the possibilities for creating a book on a specific interest.
>
> — P. Oelwein

Books about current family issues can be very relevant and helpful for students. When there is a significant event, such as the birth of a new baby or a move to a new house, a book created on the topic can serve as both an interesting story and as a transitional tool.

Teach to the Student's Book

When first reading a personal book with a student, conduct a page-by-page analysis to determine which words the student does not know. New vocabulary can be taught through the match, select, and name method. Point to words while reading to the student, and allow him to read the words he knows. Teach sentence building words such as *the, this, that, these, where, when, a, and*, in context as they appear in the book, as well as through the matching process. Allow the student to gradually build proficiency in reading the book by teaching one page at a time.

Extensions

To encourage extension, add flashcards of new words from the stories to the student's word bank. Use these cards for practice in forming sentences and reading them. Sentences in the book can be used as models, or the student can practice creating new sentences (on verbal cue, the student can select words and match them to the words in the book). Add the new words to the student's personal dictionary and to review and reinforcement activities.

The Basics of Making a Book

Books based on individual students' interests and experiences should be created frequently, using previously learned words and incorporating new words. These personalized books should have a topic and tell a story, rather than consisting of unrelated sentences and phrases. Unit books that teach words in categories (such as family, pets, animals, seasons, colors, action words, and school words) provide enrichment and useful vocabulary.

Personalized books can be simple or elaborate, as long as enhancements don't detract from the content of the book or interfere with the student's interest in reading it. Students should be encouraged to participate making their personalized books to the extent that they are able, including drawing/pasting illustrations, printing words, binding the book.

Creating a Book

- Use standard 8 ½" x 11" paper, or any size that allows ample room for one or two lines of text.
- Attach (paste, tape, draw, or copy) illustrations to the pages as available and appropriate. Use photos, drawings, or a combination of the two to illustrate the text.
- Text can be hand printed or printed on a computer. Use a font or letter size that is simple and accessible to the child, such as Ariel 45 point.
- Space words so that each is easily identified.
- Use sturdy tag board for the front and back covers of the book. Prepare the title, such as *My Family*, and encourage the student to create an illustration for the cover or to choose a picture.
- It is often useful to laminate the pages or to use page protectors.
- A school bookbinding machine is ideal for putting the pages together, but, when necessary, pages can be stapled or put in three-ring binder. A high school student may feel more comfortable with a three-ring binder; a younger child may need a smaller book with laminated pages.

Book Preparation for Students who Participate in Sign Assisted Literacy

Creating a binder is a very efficient and organized way to prepare a print book for a non-verbal student. The binder in the following example was the first print book created for a non-verbal student who loved the character Clifford, entitled *Clifford Makes a Friend*.

Creating a Binder:

1) Decorate the cover of the binder with a greeting card or any picture of the selected character.

2) Conduct a word analysis to determine which new vocabulary words the student will need to learn, then prepare word grids and flashcards. Three-hole punch the word grids and put them in the binder. Note that the flashcards have the sign diagrams beside the vocabulary words. Insert the flashcards into a page protector, binder zip pocket, or three-hole punched zip-top freezer page.

3) After the word grid section, enlarge all of the sign diagrams for the story vocabulary on the copier and glue them on to pages of card stock for the hand sign practice section. Flashcards are also matched to the sign diagrams and can be attached to the page with velcro.

4) At the end of the binder, include two review and reinforcement activities, such as lotto games (one sign lotto, one word lotto). Pull flashcards from a box or bag, read the word, and have the student place a bingo chip on the appropriate word or sign. Bingo chips, bag and word cards can also be stored in a page protector or zip pocket.

The final binder is a complete package, containing all the materials needed to teach and reinforce learning. This way of preparing and storing materials provides a visual example of a good organizational strategy.

Reading Commercial Print Books

After students have participated in reading two or three books that have been created for them, they may be ready to read print books based on subject matter that is meaningful to them, such as a special interest or favorite television character. Initially, choose books that present simple stories in clear and simple ways. Illustrations are excellent visual cues to assist the reader in comprehending the text and can remind the child that the story focuses on a special character or thing. Illustrations should be clear and easily understood. Ideally, characters and objects will be spaced widely enough to allow for easy pointing.

When choosing books, consider the following guidelines for selecting appropriate materials:
- Choose a book based on a favorite topic (such as dogs) or character (such as Thomas the Tank Engine).
- If possible, allow the student to select a book. If necessary, modify the text so that it is accessible.
- Start with simple texts, with one or two lines of print per page.
- The language of the story should be familiar to the child.

Teach students to read commercial print books following the same method as used for teaching personal experience books:
- Conduct a page-by-page analysis of the words in the book to determine which words the student does not know. Make a list of these words. Some new words can be taught in context and others can be taught through the match, select, and name method.
- Make flashcards for new words from the book so that the student can practice using them out of context and can arrange the words to make story-related sentences.

- Add new words to the student's personal dictionary and word bank.
- Have the student practice reading the story to classmates, other teachers, and family members. This provides opportunities to receive positive reinforcement and increases the student's profile as a participant in literacy.

Adapting Books

Occasionally, the student or instructor may choose a book that is too advanced or simply too challenging for the student to master at his current stage of skill development. An advanced level book may be adapted to the student's skill level in two ways:

Creating a Modified Book
- Purchase two copies of the same book: one for reading to the student, and the other to cut up to make into an adapted book. Alternatively, it may be possible to photocopy a small number of selected illustrations.
- Simplify the story structure. Keep in mind the concept of controlled vocabulary by repeating names and key phrases where possible.
- Cut out, photocopy, or scan and print out appropriate illustrations to match the new, simplified sentences.
- Print the adapted sentences and paste them, along with matching illustrations, in a small notebook or scrapbook, or in a book created with a binding machine.

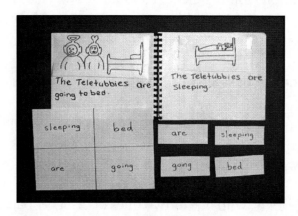

- Teach new vocabulary through the match, select, and name method.
- As the student's interest in the book increases, more sentences can be added to the adapted book.
- As part of the shared reading experience, encourage the student to recognize and read as much of the text as possible, providing ongoing praise and positive reinforcement.

Modifying Text in a Book
In some cases, it may be possible to cover the existing text with a simplified version that corresponds directly to what is occurring in the illustration. Sticky note glue may be

used to glue on flaps of paper so that modified text (using words from the student's existing sight vocabulary) covers the original text. These flaps can be easily removed with no harm to the book (see below).

Creating Communication Boards to Accompany Books

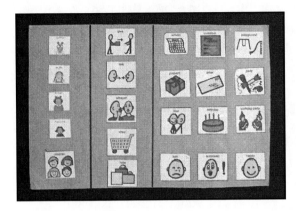 

The illustration appearing below the book in the above example shows a communication board made specifically for the story using Boardmaker (Mayer-Johnson) picture symbols. Each page of the book also has relevant picture symbols glued on, again affixed with sticky note glue. The communication board serves as a visual means for students who are non-verbal to participate in comprehension activities. It also serves as a visual prompt for students who may need some assistance with retrieving information and responding.

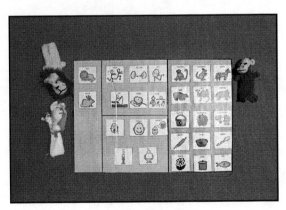

The communication board in the preceding illustration was designed specifically to match the characters and events in the children's story, *Tawny Scrawny Lion*, by Kathryn Jackson (1952). The text in this story may be too difficult for younger students to read, yet they would enjoy hearing it. A well-designed story board such as this aids with information retrieval, helps the child to keep track of events discussed in the story, and helps to strengthen the child's ability to focus and establish joint attention.

Scrapbooks

Scrapbooks enable students to gather information about a topic and keep it together in one place, mirroring how the brain compartmentalizes information and develops categorization skills. Include in the scrapbook pictures cut from magazines/ catalogues, and pictures on special topics (such as favorite TV characters), as well as pictures from common advertisements and menus. Accompany pictures with words that can, over time, be added to the student's word bank. Scrapbooks can be created about any subject, either for pleasure or academic participation, or both, and the student should actively participate in their creation.

Using Popular Television or Movie Characters

There are many popular television shows that children spend a great deal of time watching. *Thomas the Tank Engine* is a particular favorite of many children with ASD. Interest in these characters can be used to foster a child's participation in reading and related activities. The photographs below show examples of visual materials that have been created for these characters. These materials are readily available and can be used to create simple, visually engaging reading materials for students.

 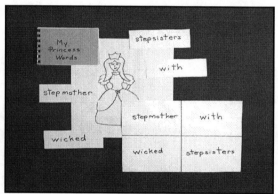

Notebooks for Conversational Scripts

Using Scripts to Develop both Reading and Conversation Skills

For students who have emerging verbal ability, the use of scripts can play an integral role in the development of both reading and verbal skills. Essentially, a script is a conversational routine—a memorized pattern of reciprocal interaction. Very often, children who are not able to verbalize spontaneously or engage in conversation are able to speak when reading. In this way, the printed word can act as a visual prompt for speech (Sundberg & Partington, 2000). A script may allow some children to verbalize more easily as they do not have to engage in the internal process of originating and processing the language required to either offer thoughts or comments or to respond to the comments of others.

Scripts can be created for various scenarios. They can be rehearsed over and over again until students are confident in the conversational routine so that participation in a particular conversation is possible. Over time, these conversations grow in number and complexity, providing practice of verbal skills. Scripts also expand students' reading vocabularies and understanding of how words relate to the activities of daily living and social interaction.

Preparing a Script:
1) Choose a routine or activity in which the student is regularly involved, such as meeting a classmate in the hall, choosing a book in the library, sitting with a classmate at lunch, going out at recess, etc.
2) Prepare a simple script of the interaction that could be expected in a particular situation. Make the conversation as natural as possible.
3) Write the script like a play:

   Mrs. Smith: Hi, Johnny. How are you today?
   Johnny: Hi, Mrs. Smith, I'm fine thanks.

4) Teach any new words involved in the conversation. Using the match, select, and name method, one is not bound by grade level reading expectations that could limit conversational potential. Any word at any grade level can be taught through this method.
5) Rehearse reading the script until the student is able to respond on his own.
6) Read the script with the student in various settings and at different times of day.
7) Introduce the routine of the script without the paper copy and encourage the student to recite it by memory.
8) Over a period of days, rehearse the script (without the paper copy) in various settings.
9) Gradually add new components/new dialogue to the script, without making changes to the printed copy, if possible.
10) See if the student is able to spontaneously respond to the new elements in the context of the familiar conversational routine.
11) If the child experiences difficulty, add the new components to the printed script and rehearse them until the child is confident in saying them without the printed script.
12) When the child has a degree of mastery over one script, prepare another. If possible, use some of the words from other conversations (controlled vocabulary).
13) Dedicate a notebook to recording conversational scripts that can be regularly reviewed.

Be patient with this process. Helping a student to build conversational skills is a lengthy process. Be sensitive to the speed at which the child is able to use reading, recall, and processing skills to develop verbal communication skills.

The mother of a six-year-old boy with Down syndrome wanted her son to use words rather than yelling when he wanted something, and to be polite.

The child read well, so the mother made sentence scripts for a variety of situations in which her son tended to yell for things, and placed them in front of him before he started yelling. For example, when he came to the breakfast table, she placed a sentence, "I want apple juice please," on the table before he had a chance to yell for juice. Rather than yell, the child would read the script and the mother responded quickly with a glass of apple juice. As he was drinking the apple juice, she showed him the sentence script, "Apple juice is delicious," and he politely read the script. The same procedure was repeated with oatmeal. The child also routinely yelled for a toy in the car, so his mother prepared a script for this situation. After reading the script just one time, he ceased yelling and started asking for the toy.

— P. Oelwein

Summary:

Once students have acquired an initial bank of vocabulary words, they need to perceive the use of these words by reading them in sentences and reading those sentences in books. This demonstrates to students that they are participating in reading along with their classmates. Students with ASD, DS, and other learning difficulties know when they have achieved something significant, and reading a book is significant. Although creating personal books takes some time at first, the goal is for skills to transfer to print books so that students are able to read for both pleasure and for information.

This journey may take place over several years. Although the long-term rewards sparked by the creation of that first book may not be immediately evident, like the farmer who plants seeds for trees he will never see in maturity, teaching these skills will ultimately make a huge difference in the lives of your students.

CHAPTER EIGHT:
READING COMPREHENSION

Mirenda (2003) states that "text comprehension requires readers to attend to word meanings and to both activate and apply background knowledge and experiences (i.e., schema) to text formation and understanding." This background knowledge and experience can generally be garnered through observation and participation in the usual events of family, social and community life.

However, the life experiences of children with Down syndrome, ASD, and other developmental disabilities are often more limited than those of typical children. Because of sensory and/or behavioral issues, they may not be able to participate in various social opportunities and events, such as going to the mall, going to a circus or seeing a movie. These students who lack certain life experiences are often successfully motivated to read by incorporating subject matter in which they are interested—and which may deviate significantly from the regular curriculum and standard classroom materials. However, when students are provided with reading material in which they are interested, that has personal relevance, and that is useful to them, they more readily participate in literacy activities and are better able to develop reading comprehension skills.

> "Some children develop a special interest in a topic or hobby and want to spend much time engaged in its pursuit or in conversation about it. This can be very useful for staff and parents, as the interest can become an incentive to engage in activities..." (Jones, 2003, p.5).

Part of the process of learning to read is developing the ability to comprehend stories and information presented in print in increasingly sophisticated ways. Again, this is an individual journey for each student. After the preliminary use of personal books (such as the *All About Me* book), stories based on favorite characters can be a useful bridge to books about characters and information that may not be as familiar to the student. The timeline for reaching the point of working with less familiar content or with non-fiction will be different for each student.

Specific Strategies for Building Skills in Reading Comprehension

The following strategies are useful for helping students develop comprehension skills:

- Beginning when children are young, provide them with information about stories as you read them, such as who is performing the action, where the events are happening.
- Model the responses that are being sought from the student: "Look, the bunny is running."
- Point to the illustrations while reading. This helps the student to understand that pointing indicates an answer. Pointing also helps to establish joint attention (both teacher and student are focused on the same illustration or words).
- Let the child respond in a slow and comfortable manner to prevent him from being intimidated by the expectation of having to respond. If he is not able to respond, rest before trying again, or move on to the next page or picture.
- Sometimes students want to read or listen to the same story over and over again. Repeated reading of familiar texts is not only acceptable, it is encouraged, as it helps to develop fluency (Mirenda, 2003). It is important, though, to make sure that the student is not simply reciting from memory, but is able to point to words as he reads them and use his finger to follow along.
- Do not bombard the student with talk. Be mindful of possible auditory processing difficulties. At this point, the goal is for the student to understand the story, not the peripheral language of discussion.
- When the student demonstrates the ability to respond to simple comprehension questions about familiar and preferred materials, introduce a new story. If the student likes the story, read it to the point of anticipation and comfort, then begin the process of demonstrating and eliciting responses.
- If a point is reached where the student balks during this activity, stop for awhile and return later with something new and enticing.
- Create story tapes that include instructions to turn the pages at the appropriate moment and provide them along with the books.
- Many commercially available learning products and toys, such as the Leap Pad™, are designed to engage children in reading. Expose students to a selection of the devices to discern if they are attracted to them.

- If it is easier for the student, provide him with his own copy of a book so he can read along while the story is read aloud to the class.
- Allow for and expect repeated readings of the passages about which questions will be asked.
- Modify questions when necessary. Factual questions are more easily answered.
- Ask questions that can be answered in a yes/no, true/false, or multiple choice format. These are much easier to answer than questions that require lengthy responses.
- Cloze (fill in the blank) exercises are useful in enabling students to recall information and indicate their understanding of story detail.
- If the student is working on answering questions based on information in a paragraph, it may be useful for him to write the number of the question beside the appropriate line or words in the paragraph. This serves as a visual guide, reminding the student where to find the answers.
- Help the student locate the requested information and have him use a highlighter pen to denote the key points, such as the main idea of a paragraph. This skill will become more and more useful as the student moves into the higher grades.

Webs and Maps

Story webs and mapping strategies are excellent visual tools for helping students plan, as well as analyze elements of a story. Several software programs provide a variety of visual formats for planning, comprehending, and writing fiction and non-fiction. These include Smart Ideas™, Kidspiration™ and Inspiration™.

When introducing webs, it is important that students understand their function and that the information presented in the web is obvious. Begin with a simple format that will allow students to discern the focus or theme, such as this "spider" web, shown below, featuring the main characters of the Thomas the Tank Engine stories.

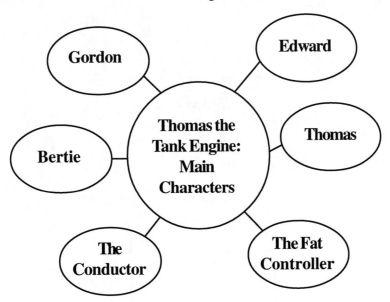

Ideally, a web would include pictures of the characters in the bubbles. Webs can be extended to other aspects and themes of a story, such as location, items used by the characters, and the sequence of events. Webs and maps can be particularly useful for non-fiction, as they allow the student to gather information and organize it visually. A web may use a vertical format for sequence, or a branch format for arranging information on a specific topic.

Branch format:

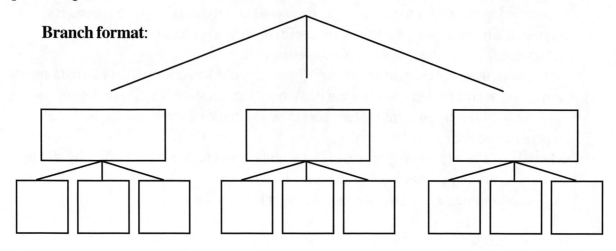

Simple story outline format:

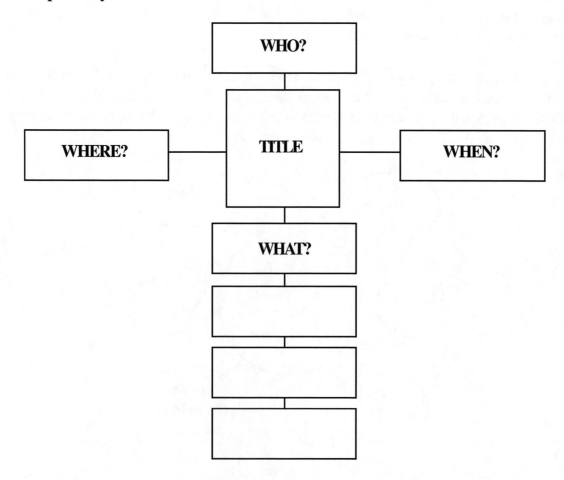

Temporal Awareness and Sequencing

Many students who have ASD and DS, as well as some students with Attention Deficit Disorder, have difficulty perceiving and understanding the passage of time and temporal concepts. Persons with autism may become "lost in time" and have significant difficulty remembering their personal experiences. Persons who have Down syndrome also report difficulties with placing themselves in time, predicting time, and remembering the sequences of events in their lives. Difficulties such as these can have a significant effect on one's ability to comprehend both real and fictional events.

If one does not perceive a sequence of events through time, then one cannot discern and comprehend causality. The perception of sequence and understanding of causality are crucial to successful reading comprehension. Building sequencing skills must therefore be an ongoing focus of the student's instruction, both at home and at school.

Photographic sequences about the child's life may be used to help develop episodic memory. Take pictures of the child moving through an activity, such as getting dressed or brushing his teeth, and input the pictures into a Power Point presentation so that the student has access to this visual representation of the desired skill or sequence.

Tools that may assist in building sequencing skills include:
- A visual schedule of activities at school and at home.
- A home/school communication book, which can be reviewed at the end of the day and the end of the week.
- Calendars denoting weekly, monthly and yearly events. Save these and review them with the child from time to time: "Remember when…"
- Photograph albums that specifically follow the child's growth and development, representing the sequence of life: baby, toddler, preschooler, kindergarten, etc. For the child with ASD or DS, the use of an album may be the only way of recalling something or remembering specific details. Small photo albums are perfect formats for storing and reviewing familiar sequences. Some photo albums include a voice output component which enables a verbal description to accompany a picture.
- Photographs of the child taken through the school year, arranged in date order, can help develop an understanding of chronological sequence.
- Videos and DVDs that record various holidays and special events. A video record of a day's tasks helps the student remember daily routines and reinforces the concept of time progressing from morning to night.
- Teach the vocabulary of time, including the words: *yesterday, today, tomorrow, past, present, future, now, later, then, long ago, once upon a time, then, minute, hour, day, week, month, year, last week, next week, awhile, soon.*

Temporal concepts that are critical to the sequencing process are beginning, middle, and end:

- Beginning: is the student able to remember and retell what happened at the beginning of a story or an event?
- Middle: the middle of a book may be difficult for a student to explain. Is the student able to recall and share some of the actions and events? Can he list and place them in sequence?
- End: is the student able to recall and tell what happened at the end of the story? Is he able to explain how the conclusion was reached? This is often the most difficult question for the student.

When teaching students to discern and determine the events in the beginning, middle and end of a story, a simple chart that provides a format for visual organization of ideas may be very helpful. (See Appendix T8.1. & T8.2. for Reading Comprehension Response Chart templates).

In the following sections, issues in reading comprehension for students with Autism Spectrum Disorders and Down syndrome are specifically addressed; however, the strategies discussed are applicable for all students who experience difficulty with reading comprehension.

Reading Comprehension: Students who have Autism Spectrum Disorders

---

Fiction vs. Non-fiction

The appreciation of fiction is a cultural value. It is not a survival skill.

Many students with special learning needs find the comprehension of fiction to be extremely difficult and have a strong preference for reading non-fiction. Whenever possible, it is important to make the accommodation of providing non-fiction materials for eliciting comprehension responses and posing information retrieval questions.

For many students with ASD, participation in reading comprehension activities poses a considerable challenge, and it is incumbent upon teachers to assist these students in deriving meaning from both fiction and non-fiction. It is critical for teachers to accept that comprehension skills may take many years to develop. In preparing Individual Education Plans and in evaluating student progress, it is useful to keep in mind that comprehension activities are often the most difficult aspect of participation in literacy for students with special needs. It is not unreasonable for goals to be conservative.

> "Higher order cognitive strategies allow for integration, inference, analysis, synthesis, creativity, negotiation, assumptions, predictions, anticipation and clarification of information. It is precisely these skills that are so profoundly affected in the learning, social and communication behaviors of children with autism" (Quill, 2000, p. 5).

Clearly, comprehension involves a significant list of higher order thinking skills and progression through this list may not be possible for all students.

The most important goal of developing students' skills in reading comprehension is to enable them to derive both meaning and enjoyment from reading. This is most easily accomplished when students are comfortable with the method of instruction and do not feel upset or threatened by the tasks they are being asked to perform.

> While many students struggle with responses beyond basic "wh" questions (who, what, when, where, why), some are able to master a deep understanding of literature. One student I worked with who has Asperger's syndrome is virtually a Tolkien scholar. He had read every book and essay by Tolkien and could discuss this work in depth and detail. He was thrilled to learn that he could actually pursue English Literature in college and that his study of Tolkien could influence his lifetime career choice.   — L. Broun

Children with ASD often cannot understand interactions, feelings and motives in "real life." Understanding the behavior of characters in books is even more difficult. The concepts of Theory of Mind and Central Coherence explain why students with ASD and other special needs often have difficulty understanding and integrating information. These concepts, as well as strategies to assist students with ASD in learning to comprehend fiction and non-fiction, are discussed below.

Theory of Mind

To have a theory of mind is to be able to attribute independent mental states to self and others in order to explain and predict behavior. The Theory of Mind explanation of autism suggests that persons with ASD lack the ability to think about thoughts and have specifically impaired social, communicative and imaginative skills (Happe, 1994). Many students with ASD are unable to understand not only the nuances of social situations, but also the reasons why people/characters behave as they do. If one combines the inability to impute thoughts and feelings to others with the previously discussed difficulties with temporal awareness and sequencing, it follows that many students with ASD, by the very nature of the disorder, may be unable to understand the actions of story characters, as well as the motivation for their behavior. These students would therefore be unable to respond accurately to comprehension questions that require higher order cognitive strategies.

Central Coherence

Frith's theory of Central Coherence (1998) is also helpful in developing an understanding of the difficulties that persons with autism experience with comprehension of both real and fictional events, as well as with understanding environmental information. Frith explains central coherence as the tendency or ability to integrate diverse information in order to construct higher level meaning in context. Central coherence allows the gist of stories or situations to be discerned and recalled easily; details are given the appropriate significance and do not overwhelm one's perception.

Students who struggle with central coherence may be unable to "see the forest for the trees." In other words, the individual may not grasp the entire picture or gist of a story, but will perhaps focus on a detail that may or may not be significant to the events or information being considered.

> A student with ASD was studying a unit on electricity with a mainstream science class. The teacher showed the students an instructional video and was impressed by how avidly his student with ASD was paying attention. He congratulated himself on presenting something that caught the student's interest and waited anxiously to ask the young man what he thought of the video. As it turned out, the student's attention had been captured by a small cartoon representation of electricity in the upper left corner of the video. The boy did not remember anything about the video content, only the presence and actions of the cartoon in the corner.
> — L. Broun

One of the major implications for students with a lack of central coherence is that they may not be able to grasp a story line, discern a theme or discover the main idea of a paragraph or passage. The latter aspect of not being able to discern central themes and main ideas will have significant implications for studying, taking tests and generally understanding what they are reading or watching.

Ongoing practice in detecting the main idea of short paragraphs or descriptive passages is necessary for students with ASD. Reading comprehension units that present short passages accompanied by multiple choice questions provide extremely useful and reasonably engaging means of assisting students in developing an understanding of theme. Initially, it may be necessary to provide students with significant guidance. Again, this is where incorporating personal and meaningful materials can be most useful. Students are more likely to attend to a story and may be more able to discern its gist if it is about people or characters that interest them.

A particular concern regarding participation in reading comprehension activities is that students with ASD, particularly Asperger's syndrome, may be penalized and receive poor marks as the result of an impairment that is inherent to their disorder. These students may prefer to read non-fiction, and allowing the use of non-fiction material for reading practice and evaluation is a fair and legitimate accommodation.

Other possible accommodations for students who have difficulty understanding and integrating information include:
- Creating short answer format questions and allowing students to point to or circle answers to accommodate communication difficulties (yes/no, true/false, and multiple choice questions);
- Allowing students to use a keyboard for written responses to accommodate motor planning problems;
- Using books or stories one or two grades below the child's reading level that are easier to understand and may allow the student to be more successful in responding to questions;
- Asking factual ("wh") questions;
- Allowing for repeated reading of passages about which questions will be asked;
- Showing video stories and pausing the video at key points to ask the child about what is happening;
- Allowing the student to take videos home to watch several times to process the language and discern and understand the sequence of events.

> On being asked why he preferred to read non-fiction, one student who has Asperger's Syndrome reported, "Well, it's true." Fiction made little sense to him and, in his mind, reading fiction did not serve a purpose.   — L. Broun

Reading Comprehension: Students who have Down Syndrome

Often, when working with students who have Down syndrome, concerns are expressed about the discrepancy between comprehension scores (generally low) and reading scores (significantly higher). This has led some educators to conclude that it is not beneficial to teach reading to students who "call words" but don't seem to comprehend what they mean. However the solution is not to withhold instruction from students with special needs, but to teach reading with an emphasis on word recognition and comprehension of meaning. Without teaching word recognition, students with DS fail to develop a skill that may be a natural strength for them, and they are put at a disadvantage in speaking, as well as in reading and writing. Most importantly, students who are not taught reading and word recognition are deprived of the foundation upon which future learning is built.

The methodological approach used to teach reading may contribute to comprehension difficulties. The Oelwein method is designed to teach a word's meaning at the time the word is first taught. Picture cards can be used to illustrate words that represent people, objects, and actions, and abstract words (that can't be illustrated) are taught in the context in which they are used. This method makes use of the child's strengths in accessing his visual memory. In addition, each word is taken through the stages of learning in which comprehension is practiced, transferred, and generalized.

Students with Down syndrome generally read for the meaning, often substituting a synonym for the printed word. For example, a student may read the word *chair*, but say "sit." Comprehension is intact—the meaning of the symbols is present, only the choice of word is incorrect. This reading error can be easily corrected by teaching the student to read the word he is substituting. When the reading material is within the student's experience and the information has meaning to him, he has a reason to remember it.

Another source of difficulty in determining the student's level of comprehension may be the method used for evaluation. For example, it is unreliable to test a student with DS using an evaluation process that consists of the teacher asking him questions (auditory input) and the student answering verbally (verbal output) because students with Down syndrome typically have difficulty with auditory processing and auditory short-term memory. These students may not process or remember the question, and may also have trouble with answering because verbal output is often the most difficult means of response for them. Tests that require writing for the output may also present a problem for students with DS who may have compromised motor function.

Some students who have Down syndrome may have no difficulties with simple comprehension. However, even students who have a talent for reading and can read just about anything may not be able to comprehend reading material if it is above their level of understanding or outside their life experience. Reading material should be at the student's level of understanding and within his experience (with challenges gradually introduced over time), regardless of his reading skills. High interest, age-appropriate books are available at each reading level. Some are original stories and some are adaptations of "chapter books" that peers are reading, written with less complexity and simpler vocabulary. In time, with maturity and ongoing practice, reading comprehension will improve as will reading scores; however higher reading scores are a fringe benefit. The real benefits are the competency and pleasure that students gain through reading.

Aaron was three when he started in the reading program. During a parent-teacher conference, Aaron's mother asked the teacher about his reading. The teacher replied, "Oh, I gave up on that! I couldn't keep up with him!"

Once children such as Aaron "break the code," it is not necessary to make specialized materials and go through the process of teaching sight words. They can move on to printed books and personalized books that provide useful information relevant to the student. The emphasis will be on comprehension.

Aaron's favorite activity was sitting in a beanbag chair and reading. He became very good scrabble player, holding is own with his father, a genetics professor.
— P. Oelwein

Checking for Comprehension

Testing or probing for recall of descriptive details in a story is not a good measure of comprehension as that information may not be truly relevant to the theme or main idea. Fiction is to be read for pleasure, and if the student enjoys reading it, the primary purpose has been served. Many stories will not be maintained in long-term memory. Discuss the story with the student rather than quizzing him on details. Talk about the happy, sad, exciting, and scary parts to encourage recall of the story. If it is determined that the student needs to and is capable of learning and remembering details of a story, allow him to read or hear the story numerous times, which will make recall easier.

It is important to recognize what skill/knowledge is being tested and to design questions that will accurately reflect the student's learning. Literacy testing may evaluate:
  • The student's recall of descriptive details,
  • Their interpretation of the character's emotions,
  • The student's perception of sequence in the story,
  • The student's understanding of the gist of the story,
  • The student's impression of how the story concluded.

When a student is not able to provide written responses (due to poor fine motor skill development and underdeveloped keyboarding skills), comprehension may be measured by having the student select correct answers using a multiple-choice format on the parts of the story which in which he displayed most interest by scribing the student's verbal answers. Whenever possible, in a testing situation, use words in the student's reading vocabulary and written at his level.

Summary:

Developing reading comprehension skills is an ongoing challenge for students with special learning needs. The instruction process should begin in the early grades, using student-centered materials. As students move along the continuum of literacy, there should be relevance in what they read. If material is too abstract, they will quickly lose interest and withdraw from the process. If comprehension questions are too challenging, again there will be withdrawal from the process. When in doubt, or when the student experiences significant difficulty, return to material that is personally relevant and meaningful or, at the least, based on personal interests. By accommodating students' learning styles and difficulties with spoken and written expression, instructors will be able to more accurately evaluate what students know.

9

CHAPTER NINE:
COMPOSITION AND CREATIVE WRITING

Composition and creative writing are important components of literacy skill development in the general education curriculum. However, the composition process can be extremely challenging for many students who have special learning needs. As with reading comprehension, the development of creative writing skills may take place over a span of years and should be planned for accordingly.

For students with special learning needs, it may be necessary to question how useful composition and creative writing skills will ultimately be in the "big picture" of their academic lives. How useful is it to persevere in teaching a difficult skill that may have little relevance to the student's future? Is it more useful to engage in other, more relevant skill-building activities? Keeping in mind the issue of relevance, it may be prudent to focus on aspects of composition (other than writing stories), such as keeping a diary or writing a letter, that will be most valuable. The best course of action for students who struggle with composition and creative writing is usually to use a specialized approach for instruction, modify goals, and allow for alternative means of expression.

The following strategies provide useful activities and guidelines for helping students with special learning needs develop writing skills.

Drawing
Often, the first way in which children are able to engage in story telling/story composition is through drawing pictures, making drawing an important component in the creative writing process. Many teachers and parents ask their student or child to tell them about what is happening in a picture they have drawn or painted. The adult will ask questions to elicit further details about the story behind the picture. Through the drawing, the child is

making a symbolic representation of his ideas or story, which is the beginning of the story composition process. Drawing is also helpful for developing and practicing motor skills that will be useful when learning to write.

To promote drawing, have the following materials available:
- Felt pens and markers, pencils (colored as well as standard), crayons, and a generous supply of paper (preferably paper that is being recycled, or newsprint);
- Chalk (white and colored) and a sturdy chalkboard;
- Dry erase markers and a whiteboard;
- Paint and easel with paper.

Many children with ASD, DS, and other learning difficulties can learn to draw at any stage, and children soon realize that their marks mean something. It is important to model how to draw on a daily basis. By observing the drawing of squares, circles, squares, simple faces, etc., students can, through **imitation**, gradually work towards making their lines have discernible meaning. This is called **imitative model drawing**.

To initiate imitative model drawing, set up a large piece of paper, oriented horizontally, and draw a vertical line down the middle to divide the page into two equal parts. Use one side of the page to model the drawing of the shape, and indicate to the child by gesture the expectation: for him to make the same kind of line. This is also a good opportunity to practice turn-taking.

Common first lines and shapes include:

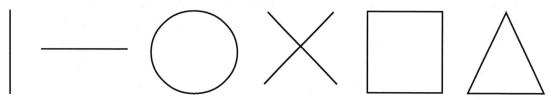

Once the student has mastered the ability to copy simple lines, it will be possible for him to begin to make representative drawings.

When a child offers a piece of paper on which he has drawn lines, ask him to explain it. Asking the child, "Tell me about your picture," is likely to elicit more language than simply asking "What is this?" which implies that his drawing is unrecognizable. Even if the form is not recognizable, the picture has meaning for the child and he needs the opportunity to explain or share that meaning. If the child is non-verbal, simply say, "You made a wonderful picture."

It may be helpful to present the student with a selection of photographs or picture symbols of preferred persons, cartoon characters, toys and common environmental items to which he can point in order to indicate what he has drawn. Photographs, pictures and picture symbols can be minimized and mounted on a piece of tag board and then laminated. A board of this kind can be used, not only for drawing practice, but also as inspiration for composition and conversation. Remember to use the word *picture* regularly when engaged in pencil and paper tasks with the child.

Imitative model drawing is an excellent strategy for helping students build motor skills and expand the range of lines, shapes and forms that they are able to draw. Furthermore, participation in drawing provides opportunities for students to learn a range of new vocabulary words, such as the following:
- *Start, stop;*
- *Down, up, across, around, curve, straight, below, above, on;*
- The names of the colors and shapes;
- The names of marking tools and equipment involved in drawing and other art-related activities.

Other activities, such as coloring, tracing, and connect-the-dots games, can also enhance fine motor abilities and prepare students for printing. The primary goal is for the student to understand that his marks on paper have meaning and that he can use this medium for communication.

Moving to Words: Beginning the Process

As students acquire more vocabulary words, increase their spelling skills and develop an understanding of simple sentence structure, they are ready to use words to express their ideas and compose stories about themselves and their interests, as well as share information about what they are learning.

Printing and Writing Skills

An integral aspect of literacy is the development of written communication skills, including the physical aspects of print production. Many students with special learning needs find it more difficult to send a message, either verbal or written, than to receive it. Visual learners who can read may process and remember a written message or response better than a spoken one due to weaknesses in auditory short-term memory. In addition, some children with special needs have speech problems that make it difficult for them to be understood, and writing gives them a means to communicate and express themselves clearly and effectively. Therefore, it is especially important for students with speech problems to be able to write down information, either by handwriting or keyboarding. The decision as to whether to teach printing or keyboarding is based on the individual child's abilities and willingness to use a particular writing instrument.

While some children with special learning needs, such as Down syndrome, can read at levels that exceed their mental age, they will not be able to write at a level beyond the developmental stage of their fine-motor skills. It is important that these students not be bogged down or overwhelmed with printing or writing, struggling to form the letters and forgetting the message. Just as concentrating on sounding out words interferes with comprehension, concentrating on forming letters with a pencil interferes with thinking about and composing the message. For students who are unable to handwrite, other options are available. *The ability to write with pencil and paper is not a prerequisite for composition and creating writing.*

Functional Writing

As with reading, the technicalities of writing are not as important as the purpose it serves. If the student's ability to print benefits him (i.e., if he is able to read his own notes, papers, and journals and communicate to others using the written word), then his writing is functional. Also, as with reading, it is important for the student to have an immediate and ongoing use for engaging in the print process. The instructor should emphasize communication rather than "correctness" in technique. When daily writing activities are meaningful, skills will improve with ongoing coaching and practice.

Cursive Writing

Some children with special needs can easily transfer to cursive writing. Cursive writing skills will allow students to sign their names and read cursive text. Once students are proficient in cursive writing, the style is more efficient than printing.

For students who are able to print and/or use a keyboard, the decision will eventually have to be made as to whether or not they will benefit from learning how to write in cursive style. If the students' needs are best met by keyboarding, for instance, then instruction time may be more profitably spent engaging in other academic activities, such as practicing keyboarding skills, reading, or mathematics.

Several excellent programs that teach students to write letters and number are available, including:
- *The Sensible Pencil* (ATC Learning, LLC, P.O. Box 43795, Birmingham, AL 35243, 800-633-8623): designed for use by young children and children with neurological, learning or cognitive disabilities.
- *Callirobics*: handwriting exercises set to music. This program provides templates for letter formation and for pre-skill development of pencil manipulation skills. See www.callirobics.com.
- *Handwriting Without Tears*: a developmentally-based program with multisensory teaching aids and methods. See www.hwtears.com.
- *Learn to Print and Draw*: a visual and kinesthetic program designed by occupational therapists S. Wahl and S. Sutton. See www.ot-shirleysutton.com.

• The website *http://teachers.santee.k12.ca.us/carl* offers a wide variety of educational worksheets and resources, including a detailed printing and cursive writing program with worksheets.

The Keyboarding Alternative:

Many students experience difficulty with the physical process of printing and cursive writing and are better able to respond to comprehension questions if they do not have to engage in printing or writing. For students with a wide range of learning differences, printing and writing skills are very weak and may interfere with academic performance. Nonetheless, many individuals who are not able to print efficiently are able to do other things with their hands very well, such as play musical instruments, sew, draw or manipulate tools and machinery.

The persistent inability to form letters correctly and quickly is called dysgraphia (printing), or dyscriptia (writing). It is not uncommon for students with ASD or DS to struggle with producing legible print. A student with dysgraphia may:
• Focus more energy on the printing process than on thinking about the content and quality of his response;
• Write as few words as possible to answer a question so as to minimize the physical printing process (e.g., if a sentence is asked for, a few words may be given; if a paragraph is requested, the student may produce a sentence or two).

For students who struggle with producing print, intellectual or cognitive processing takes a back seat in the composition process to the difficult physical process of putting pencil to paper. Thus, the quality and quantity of response is reduced and, over time, the student will become habituated to thinking and writing in as few words as possible, thereby significantly limiting the thinking process. When a student is thinking about how to express himself in as few words as possible, his intellectual energy is diverted away from producing reasoned, thoughtful responses.

It is important to take into consideration the likelihood of dysgraphia or dyscriptia when determining the rubric by which to evaluate students with special needs. Too often, the visual presentation of work influences the perception of the student's ability, even though how legibly one prints or writes is completely irrelevant to learning and intelligence.

At the International Meeting for Autism Research in June, 2006, Dr. Marcel Just discussed his recent neurological research on individuals with ASD. He and his research team found that in the brains of persons with autism, the performance of a multi-process task results in a reduction of the available resources (i.e., blood/oxygen supply) for each component. Thus, the individual may be less able to focus on or effectively complete the composite elements of a task. As more steps are added, there is a decrease in the coordination of the affected brain areas.

In today's technological society, we are fortunate to have a suitable alternative to the pencil for producing writing: the keyboard. There are several engaging and entertaining keyboarding programs available, both commercially and in schools. This critical life skill should be cultivated as early as possible. The important thing is to recognize when a student's struggles with the pencil are interfering with his intellectual output and to provide the alternative of the keyboard. Instead of insisting the child practice printing, allow him to practice keyboarding. Take the pencil out of the process and see what happens. With time and practice at the keyboard, there may be a significant improvement in the student's ability to compose answers and respond to other "writing" tasks.

"The need to handwrite work can add extra pressure. It often takes a large amount of concentration to write legibly and therefore the child's focus is moved from their work to their writing. Having a computer available in the place of work and making it possible to word process may help" (M. Winter, 2003, p. 71).

Writing Non-Fiction: A Critical Component of Composition

As with all other aspects of literacy discussed in this book, the composition process should begin by incorporating ideas that are personal and relevant to the child and his experience. For some students, writing about things they have learned or about information based on fact will be highly preferable to creating stories. Some of the many writing projects that allow students to demonstrate skills, including the ability to organize information are outlined below.

Instructional Sequences

Ask the student to think about the steps necessary to perform simple tasks (conduct his own task analysis), then have him write the steps of the sequence in order. Tasks such as brushing teeth, getting dressed, and making a sandwich, are examples of reasonably simple activities for which a student can write step-by-step instructions.

Individual Research Projects across the Curriculum

Assign students individualized research projects, requiring them to gather and organize information on specific topics in which they are interested. Learning to prioritize main ideas and organize paragraphs appropriately is an important skill across all subject areas. Webs and maps are particularly useful as they provide visual formats for organizing information.

Journal Writing

Daily or weekly journal writing is a valuable component of many literacy programs. Students are instructed to write about their weekly activities or a special event that has occurred at home or at school, using words from their individual sight word vocabularies. If the student wishes to use new words, make note of these words and teach them through the match, select, and name process and add them to his word bank and personal dictionary. As the student progresses through vocabulary and sentence building activities, journal entries will become longer and more sophisticated in content and sentence structure.

The Home/School Communication Book

Communication between school and home should occur on a daily basis, and can be facilitated by using a home/school communication book that the student helps prepare. The book features several categories, including clothing, weather, date, home activities, school activities, and rules. Each category can be tracked on a separate page which may feature Mayer-Johnson™ picture symbols or other pictograms, photographs, and/or words. The student records information in each category using picture symbols, tick marks, stampers (such as bingo dabbers), and/or words.

Many students (particularly students with ASD) find that visual schedules help them know the order of activities that will take place during their day. Relating a student's schedule to the daily home reporting process both reinforces the schedule and involves the child directly in communication with parents. Set aside time at the end of each day to review the events of the day before the student goes home. The child can mark the activities and a supervisory adult can note any pertinent details. It is therefore important to familiarize the family with the home/school notebook process. Stress that it will take no more than a few moments in the evening to prepare the notebook and that it may help the child recall events accurately.

Photographs of the student involved in activities at school or at home can provide an excellent stimulus for information retrieval and communication. Take a series of pictures of the child throughout the week and transfer them to a CD-ROM. This can help the child to make links between the home and school environments, provide topics for conversation at home, and give parents a "visual record" of some of their child's experiences at school. (It is important to keep in mind that customarily permission must be given for photos of other children to be taken. Usually a form is sent home for parents to sign that would outline the intended use of the pictures.)

Students who have printing or keyboarding skills should be encouraged and guided to print or type a short message (even one word) to go into their communication books daily. This may start out as the name of a subject, such as *math*, but can eventually become more lengthy and detailed. As skills develop, the student should take on more responsibility for reporting events at school as one of his written language or composition activities.

Diaries
A diary can be an extremely useful tool for developing memory retrieval skills. A diary is much like a journal; however, it is written with the understanding that the content is not for evaluation or for sharing with others unless the writer agrees. Consistent recording of simple and special daily events can make the writing process meaningful to the student and provide a cherished record when the student is older.

Lists
Many students enjoy making lists of activities or tasks. Pre-plan and pre-teach vocabulary necessary for this activity. As soon as the student has sufficient vocabulary to participate in the process, begin working with him to make simple lists. Preferred topics for list-making include:
- Favorite foods
- Holidays
- Birthdays
- Inventories of belongings
- Friends to whom valentines (or other cards) will be sent
- Shopping lists for groceries

Several years ago, one of my students with ASD was feeling quite depressed. He had excellent verbal skills and was able to express his feelings very clearly. I suggested that he make a list of all the things in his life that made him happy and read it whenever he was feeling down. He took this task very seriously and made a long and wonderful list of all the good things in his life.

Not only did this list actually help to shift his mood, it also started a lifelong practice of list-making for everything—his videos and DVDs, favorite foods, his clothing, shopping lists for his parents, life skills activities at school, and so on. While this student carried list-making to an extreme, it provided him with a valuable organizational tool that he enjoyed using.   — L. Broun

Descriptive Writing

Descriptive writing is an important skill for students, and one that will allow them to grow as writers and transition from non-fiction to story writing. Before engaging in the writing process, students must have sufficient descriptive words in either their spoken, written, and/or signed vocabularies, as well as their sight word reading vocabularies. When spelling questions arise, refer students to their personal dictionaries or allow them to copy words from a prepared example.

Descriptive writing assignments:
• The student describes an object or objects that are personal and familiar to him, using his vocabulary words. Begin by instructing the student to provide verbal or signed descriptions, or have him point to a picture symbol or printed word to respond to descriptive questions.
• The student describes photographs of himself and his family members. Suggest that the student describe where he was when the photo was taken, what he was doing, what he was wearing, what is happening, etc. Gradually introduce pictures of the larger environment for the student to describe.
• The student describes a favorite story illustration. Allow the student to choose an illustration, then copy or scan that illustration and glue or staple it into his composition book.

When and if he is able, encourage the student to write the description in his descriptive writing notebook or type it on the computer. At first, responses as simple as one word may be appropriate. As the student's skills develop, he should be encouraged to compose more complex descriptions, such as a detailed paragraph (provided it is within his capability to do so).

Fiction

Composing Stories

By the time students are ready to begin story writing, they will have been exposed to many books, both commercial and student-specific, as well as movies and television shows. Despite this familiarity with stories, the act of composing a story can pose a considerable challenge. Students may have difficulty making up characters and events, in which case they should be prompted to write stories about themselves, their families, friends, and/or pets. An imaginary character may be too much of a leap. Initial efforts may be comprised of only two or three lines. All efforts must be praised as the student builds confidence.

Just as with reading comprehension, story writing requires students to pay attention to the basic elements of a story, which can be recorded in chart form (see Appendix for reproducibles T9.1. Basic Story Element Template, and T9.2. My Story Template) before the student begins to write. Students may also use this chart format to draw the elements of the story.

Planning how to begin the story and how the action will proceed is crucial and speaks to the need for understanding sequence. Listing the elements of the sequence in chart form can be very helpful (See Appendix for T9.3. Story Sequence Chart). Further visual analysis can include a chart to clarify how the story will begin, how it will end, and what will happen in the middle. This chart can also be used as a tool to help students analyze information in the reading comprehension process.

Beginning	Middle—the action	Ending

As a student gathers information about what he wants to include in his story, he may need significant help with integrating components, particularly with first efforts and as expectations become more complex. At this stage, if the student is not able to print, write, or type his story independently, the teacher can write it down for him or utilize a scribe. Content should not be omitted because of difficulties with fine motor skills or not knowing how to use a keyboard (this further reinforces the need for learning to use a computer keyboard and a word processing program efficiently).

John, a mainstreamed sixth grade student with high-functioning autism, would often become hysterically upset before or during creative writing periods. He was frightened by the prospect of having to make up people and events, therefore the teacher encouraged him to write stories about his family and classmates. His stories usually focused on real, daily events although, as time went on, he would occasionally add a fictional element. As he progressed through middle school, he became more confident in writing and ventured to the imaginary, often loosely basing his stories on movie themes and books he had read.
— L. Broun

Comic Book Format

Some students may find it easier and more enjoyable to first draw their stories and then add text. The finished product is akin to a comic book, with illustrations and corresponding narrative (in speech bubbles and/or text box). Provide students with a standard comic book template within which to work (See Appendix for T9.4. Comic Book Format Template).

Jonathan was a non-verbal, five-year-old boy with a diagnosis of autism. He engaged in many perseverative behaviors centered around his passion for cars and trucks, such as making engine noises, gear-changing sounds, etc. Over time, he developed verbal skills; however, despite ongoing work to develop reading skills, his short-term memory was very weak and he was not able to recognize words or letters from one day to the next.

Recognizing his difficulty with acquiring literacy skills, I decided to teach Jonathan to draw by demonstrating how to draw a simple car shape approximately one hundred times (at his request). Finally, one day I offered him the pencil and he was able to replicate the shape. That was the crucial moment in his development. He realized that he could draw and from then on, part of each day was dedicated to drawing practice. He chose drawing as his leisure activity and we allowed him extra time and whatever materials he chose in order to engage in this process.

While Jonathan was not able to read or write, over time he was able to take a piece of chart paper, divide it into twelve sections with a ruler, number the sections and then proceed to draw an intricate story in cartoon form. The stories were well sequenced and very entertaining. He was able to explain some of the story action verbally although his verbal skills were still emerging. Despite the lack of verbal or written language, through drawing he was able to create and to demonstrate an understanding of story structure. This is literacy.

— L. Broun

Summary:

Composition and creative writing may take many forms other than actual story writing. Keeping a journal or a diary or learning to make lists can be justifiably included in the student's goal profile of his Individual Education Plan. For some students, composition based in non-fiction may be a good starting point for writing, while for others, story creation may be a pleasure. In both situations, students need to be able to determine the main ideas they want to communicate and present those ideas clearly and sequentially, using grammar to the best of their ability. The goal is to make composition meaningful, relevant to students' experiences, and useful.

This strength-based approach to literacy mandates that care be taken to avoid pressuring students to perform in their particular areas of weakness. Writing can be very frustrating for some students, and if there is too much emphasis on printing practice and proper letter formation, some students may lose motivation to try to write or may engage the teacher in a power struggle that diverts the attention from the purpose of writing. If students become frustrated when dealing fine motor and print production difficulties, they may develop avoidance behaviors that interfere with progress in their area of strength: reading.

Learning to manipulate a writing instrument successfully may not be possible for all students. Those students who are unable to print words can participate in writing through using a computer and typing words. Instruction should therefore be individualized, teaching students to write/type and spell the words they use most often. Allow students to progress at their own pace, using the method that is most efficient for them. Motivated and cooperative students who have the readiness skills and ability do well are able to make progress using systematic, comprehensive writing programs.

PART III

WORDS:

WORKING FROM THE WHOLE TO THE PARTS

10

CHAPTER TEN:
PHONICS: THE ALPHABET AND SOUND/SYMBOL ASSOCIATIONS

The top-down approach of the Oelwein method for developing sight word recognition skills uses students' pre-established sight word vocabularies to teach phonemic awareness and decoding skills, enabling students to participate in regular classroom phonics-based programs and further develop their reading skills. When taught in the context of words that are meaningful, the letters are no longer isolated and abstract symbols, but can be perceived as the building blocks of words.

Students with special learning needs who have had success learning whole words through the Oelwein method are generally successful learning the alphabet and sound/symbol associations using this same method, beginning with the match, select, and name process.

> **Phonemic awareness**: the ability to reflect on and manipulate the individual speech sounds (phonemes) in a word.
>
> **Phonological awareness**: the ability to reflect on and manipulate chunks of sounds that are smaller than the word. Syllable awareness (and single word segmentation), rhyme awareness and phonemic awareness are all types of phonological awareness.
>
> **Phonics**: a method of instruction that teaches the relationships between and among letters and sounds. (Scarborough & Brady, 2002)

Introducing Letters

Begin by introducing the first letter of the words in students' sight vocabularies, starting with their names and the names of their family members. The names *Abby, Mommy, Daddy,* and *Bob*, are used in the example provided.

Stage 1: Acquisition
Procedures for teaching letter names

Objective: The student will match, select, and name upper- and lowercase letters *A, M, D*, and *B*:

Materials: Personal alphabet book and alphabet flashcards.

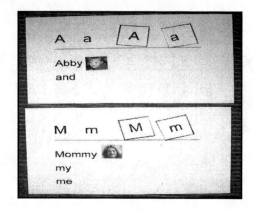

Creating students' personal alphabet books requires the following simple steps:

• Write the title on a cover made of cardstock or similar material: *"Abby's A, M, D, B Book."*
• Create a page for each letter.
• Print the upper- and lowercase form of the featured letter at the top of the page (*A,a; M,m; D,d*; and *B,b*).
• Under the featured letter, print the reading vocabulary words that have the letter in the initial position (add new words as they are added to the student's vocabulary).
  ○ On the *A,a* page, *Abby* and *and*
  ○ On the *M,m* page, *Mommy*
  ○ On the *D,d* page, *Daddy*
  ○ On the *B,b* page, *Bob* and *book*
• For children who are not interested in books without pictures, paste a small photo, line drawing, or illustration of the sign for the word.
• Make matching alphabet flashcards with the upper- and lowercase forms of the letter on separate cards (letters should appear on flashcards the same size as the letters in the book); clip flashcards to the appropriate pages.

Discriminate and name upper- and lowercase letters: Match, Select, and Name

Upper- and lowercase forms of letters are introduced and taught at the same time so that the student learns that letters exist in two forms and will not be confused when the letter changes form in another case: *A* and *a*, *B* and *b*, *D* and *d*, *E* and *e*, *G* and *g*.

- Read the first page, pointing to the letter and words as you read, "*B* for *Bob* and *ball*," emphasizing the b sound.

- **Match:** Give the student the uppercase *B* flashcard, and say, "Put the big *B* (flashcard) on the big *B* (on the page)." Give her the lowercase *b* and say, "Put the little *b* on the little *b*." If the student is older, the terms upper- and lowercase may be used instead of big and little. Individualize to match the student's ability and age.

- **Select**: Put the upper- and lowercase flashcards on the table, and ask, "Where's the big *B?*" and, "Where's the little *b?*"

- **Name**: Hold up the uppercase *B* flashcard and say, "This is the big___" and let her say or sign the name of the letter and match the *B* flashcard with the *B* on the page. Hold up the lowercase *b* flashcard and say, "This is a little___" and let her say or sign the name of the letter and match it to the lowercase *b* on the page.

- **Match letters to the letters in words**: Ask the student to take the big *B* (flashcard) and match it with the big *B* in *Bob* (on the page); then ask her to take the little *b* (flashcard) and put it on the little *b* in the word *ball* (on the page).

- **Repeat with next letters:** Repeat the same match, select, and name procedures with the next letter, *M, m* for *Mommy*. Ask the student to find the big *M* in *Mommy* and the little *m*'s in *Mommy*.

When the student has matched, selected, and named upper- and lowercase forms of two letters in her book, teach her to discriminate between these two letters; as more letters are taught, increase the choices to as many as five letters at a time.

Materials: Upper- and Lowercase Lotto game

- Make a lotto game board with two columns. Laminate and use a dry erase marker.
- In the first space of the left column, print the word *big*; in the right column print the word, *little* (for older students use *uppercase* and *lowercase* or *capital* and *lowercase*).
- Print the letters in the order that they are introduced, with the uppercase form in the *big* column and the lowercase form in the *little* column.

The Process
- **Match:** The student matches upper- and lowercase letter flashcards to exposed letters on the lotto game board
- **Select**: She points to the appropriate letter on verbal cue, "Where is the big *S*? Big *M*? Little *s*? Little *m*?"
- **Name:** She says the name of the letter when prompted, and then matches it to the letter on the card (she does not need to say or sign *big* or *little*, just name the letter and match it to the correct case).
- **Add additional letters**: Add letters, one at a time, as they have been introduced, and increase to as many as five choices. Make a new lotto game for each set of letters.

Teaching Vowels
The student's readiness to learn the concept of vowels is important. If vowels are introduced and the student indicates that she is not interested or does not understand, put vowels aside and try again later. There is no hurry. Some visual learners never understand phonics and become frustrated whenever they are presented. Pressing the issue may cause the student to engage in avoidance activities. Reading is the student's goal and phonics is only a tool to reach that goal. If the student can't use the tools, they are useless to her. She can rely on another tool that works well for her: the match, select, and name process.

The following process will make learning vowels simple and fun for the child:
- **Introduce a vowel** when the situation presents itself in the student's alphabet book.
  ○ If the *A* word is *Abby,* you will say "*A* for *Abby,*" emphasizing the short sound, teaching her to associate the letter *A* with the sound of the name, *Abby*. When a word such as *ape* is added, introduce the concept that the letter *A* has two sounds. Subsequent *A* words can then be sorted by whether or not they have long or short vowel sounds.
- **Long vowels say their own name:** Tell her that sometimes vowels say their own names in words. In the word *Abby*, the letter A says "ah;" but in *ape* it says its *own name*, "ay."
- **Repeat with other vowels**, as the situation presents itself.
- As the student reads her books, flashcards, and games, she goes on a hunt for *a*'s that say their own name within the words, as well as those in the initial position. Feel free to introduce and use this concept any time it will be helpful to the child.

Alphabet Probe
- Flash the letter flashcards, one at a time; student reads the letter—just the name—does not have to discriminate upper- and lowercase.
- Sort flashcards as the student reads them, making two piles—one for those read correctly and the other for those read incorrectly.
- Student charts number of words correctly read on a graph.
- Student's graph can have a two columns for each day: one for big letters read, one for little letters read.
- **Add letters to the probe** as they are taught. For some students it is preferable to keep the number of letters to ten or fewer, adding and dropping letters as new letters are introduced; or, all letters can stay in the probe until the student is proficient reading them, if this is not too tedious a task. Always be aware of the student's attitude at the worktable; if participation in these tasks is not fun for the student, relax the approach, perhaps using the probe just once a week. If a student does not respond well to a task, it very likely means that it has little meaning to her or is too challenging.

Sequence of the Alphabet

Many students who have good visual memories will have no trouble learning the sequence of letters. The challenge lies in conveying to them that this sequence has a useful application (alphabetization) that provides an efficient means of sorting and accessing information.

It is not immediately necessary for beginning readers to know the alphabet sequence, therefore it is not necessary, nor is it recommended, that students be taught to memorize the sequence before they can actually make use of it. When they do need it, there are simple accommodations that can be provided to teach this important lesson, such as having a printed sequence available to which they may refer. The following simple activities can aid in teaching the alphabet sequence:

Sing the "ABC Song"
- Provide ongoing exposure to the "ABC Song," even before the student learns the alphabet. Sing it to and with him and give him a tape to play, even if you have to make the tape yourself. This allows the student to hear the sequence and, even more importantly, the names of letters.
- Tape an alphabet strip to the student's desk or at his place at the table. Alphabet strips show both upper- and lowercase forms of letters with lines and arrows indicating how to write the letter. These are commonly available ready-made in school supply stores.
- When singing the song, use the alphabet strip and point to each letter as you sing it. Hold the note of the letter that has been introduced: "A Beeeee C Deeeee E F G; H

Iiiiiii J K L Mmmmm N O P; Q R Sssssss T U V; W U X Y and Z." If necessary, help the student point to the letters while you sing them.

• Next, stop singing the letters the student knows and let him sing the letter as you point until he can sing the entire song.

Magnetic and other easy-to-manipulate letters:

• The student follows the model of an alphabet strip and places magnetic letters in order. Many chalkboards are magnetized. It is also possible to purchase small, magnetized whiteboards that the student can use at his desk.

• There are many alphabet inset puzzles commercially available that provide a self-correcting way to reinforce alphabet sequence. It is important, however, that the student attend to recognition of the letter, with prompting if necessary, otherwise using this kind of puzzle is simply a visuospatial exercise.

Provide visual exposure at home and school:

• In the classroom, the alphabet should be posted so that it is easily visible to the child.

• At home, the alphabet can be displayed any place the parents choose, such as the child's bedroom (on the wall or on the ceiling above his bed), family room, or on the refrigerator door.

Stage 2: Practice to Fluency - Activities to make practice and review interesting and fun.
Lotto Games

Letter/Word Lotto

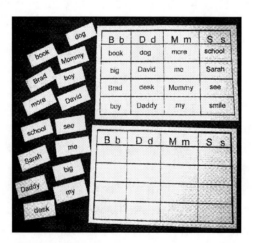

• Make a lotto game card that has as many as four columns across and write upper- and lowercase letters in the spaces across the top (make a copy of this blank one to be used for sorting).

- In the columns under each letter, print the words in the student's reading vocabulary that have the letter in the initial position.
- Use the student's set of flashcards to play the game.
- Student draws a flashcard and identifies the first letter.
- Student finds the letter at the top of the column.
- Student scans down the column to find and match the word.

Sorting-by-Letter Lotto
- Use a lotto game card with only a letter (both cases) at the top of each column; leave the spaces below blank.
- Students sort the words, placing each under the appropriate letter.
- Students can also sort pictures of people and objects (or the actual objects) by initial sound under the appropriate letter.

Alphabet Basketball
- Tape a letter (upper- and lowercase) onto each of four baskets (waste baskets or whatever containers are available).
- Students toss bean bags into baskets, taking turns if there is more than one player.
- Students score one point for making a basket; one point for naming (saying/signing) the letter; one point for saying a word that starts with the letter (*S—S* for *Sarah*).

Alphabet Bowling
- Tape letters to large plastic bottles (one letter per bottle).
- Students toss balls or bean bags to knock over the bottles.
- One point is earned for knocking over a bottle; one point for naming the letter; one point for saying a word that starts with the letter.

Alphabet Hunting
This is an enjoyable game to play at home. The objective is for the student to identify objects that start with specific letters and practice saying words that start with that sound. This activity will help with articulation and increase spoken vocabulary, as well as accentuate awareness of the sounds in words. For students who are non-verbal, this provides an excellent activity for reinforcing hand signs for the letters.
- Materials: Self-sticking notes (or cards or paper about 3" x 3" and tape) and a wide felt marker.
- Look through the house for words that start with the targeted letter, such as *s*. "*S (s)* is for *sofa*." Stick the note to the sofa.
- Stick notes on all things in the house that begin with *s*. For example, in the kitchen, ask the child: "Which one starts with *s* like *sofa*?"
- Continue going through the house, encouraging the child to find things himself as he catches on.

- When the child passes by objects without flagging them, help him review by saying, "*S* for _____" and let him fill in the blank. Or, "*Sink*, it starts with _____."
- Add another letter, such as *M* for *Mommy*. The child can stick an *M* on mirrors, money, mantle, etc. Progress to *D* for *Daddy*, and help the child find the household items starting with *D*, such as *door, desk, drawer, dryer, dress*, etc. Stick the letter *D* on these objects.
- In some cases, you will need to find pictures of objects for the letter. Tape the pictures onto surfaces, such as doors, at the child's level.

Alphabetize the Word Bank

As the student learns to recognize letters, teach him to organize the words in his word bank by filing them under the initial letter:
- Use a simple 5" x 3" file card box to make the word card file. Make vertical tab cards to indicate the letter to be filed (in both upper- and lowercase).
- Flashcards should be able to be easily removed from and returned to the file.
- As new letters are introduced, add them to the file.
- The student can look up words in his word bank, requiring him to think about what letter each word starts with.
- The student can use his alphabetical word file to look up the spelling of a word or to use the word in a particular sentence.

Make an Alphabet Book
- The student cuts out and pastes the letter (upper- and lowercase of each letter) to the top of the page of a standard scrap book, one letter per page.
- The student then cuts out letters from newspapers, magazines and other sources, sorts them, and pastes them onto the appropriate pages. He can also paste pictures of objects or persons whose names start with the letter.
- Finding pictures of objects that start with the featured letter can be a good opportunity for the student to work with a peer, sibling or parent.

Stage 3: Transfer
Recognizing Letters in Different Presentations

At this stage, the student should be able to recognize and discriminate letters printed in both upper- and lowercase in different fonts, sizes, colors, and on different surfaces. The computer provides a fast and efficient way to either create materials or provide an alternate visual presentation of words and letters on the monitor screen. Students can also practice reading letters made of different materials, such as Scrabble ™ tiles, letters in puzzles, plastic letters, and letters on ABC blocks, as well practice making letters with play dough, pipe cleaners and other craft materials.

If the student experiences significant difficulty at the transfer stage, the match, select, and name approach can be used to help the child to "see" that words/letters are the same, even when presented in different ways.

Stage 4: Generalization
Consolidation of Letter Recognition Skills
The student who has mastered the skill of consolidating letter recognition has embedded the letters in his long-term memory and is able to recognize them in any format in any context. Continued practice reinforces learning.

Summary:
The stages of learning to recognize letters is the same as learning to recognize words. Since knowing the letters and their sounds is not a prerequisite for learning to read using the Oelwein method, letters are taught after whole words (top-down approach); however, in the evolution of a student's decoding skills, it will be critical to know letters and develop skills in phonics.

One of the most important elements in teaching the alphabet is making the letters meaningful by teaching them in the context of words already in the student's sight vocabulary. While some students come to this process readily, others may need additional incentive, such as playing the games and engaging in the activities described in this chapter. For all students, ongoing review and reinforcement will play an important role in developing and consolidating both word attack and spelling skills.

11

CHAPTER ELEVEN:
PHONICS: TEACHING WORD FAMILIES

Learning how word families work often "breaks the code" of reading for students. They discover that one letter can change a word, and they learn to blend the sounds together to read the whole word. This skill will help students generalize previously learned words, and will also help them learn new words more quickly.

When to teach

For visual learners, word families are best taught when the student has 50 to 100 words in his sight vocabulary and recognizes most letters. However these are general guidelines, and it is important to assess each student individually to determine if he is ready to learn word families. Children who grasp the concept generally find word family activities to be enjoyable. If the student does not respond to instruction and/or shows a lack of interest, discontinue for the time being and continue with his regular reading activities. Introduce word family activities again later, but be aware that some students may not be able to understand the concept and will learn all their reading vocabulary through whole word sight recognition.

Applying the top-down approach

To teach word families using the top-down approach, begin by introducing short-vowel consonant families, such as *at, an, en, ug, ig,* and *oy.* Proceed by engaging students in the match, select, and name process for each family. This process can be followed to teach all short vowel-consonant families as well as other concepts such as blends, prefixes, and suffixes. The following example introduces the *at* family.

Stage 1: Acquisition—the "at" family
Teach the family word as a sight word
- Match, select, and name *at* using the two *at* flashcards
- The word *at* is treated as a short vowel-consonant sound here. Tell the child, "This says *at*."
- Teach the word family (*cat, rat, bat, sat, mat* and *hat*) as you would teach sight words using the match, select, and name method, introducing four words at a time.
- Show the student the *at* in each word and tell him that these words belong to the *at* family. Ask him to locate and point to the *at* in each word.
- Point out that each word starts with a different letter. Say the sound of the first letter and blend it with the family sound to form a word: say the hard *c* sound, "(k), k-at, *cat*."
- Some students with auditory processing problems may have trouble with the initial sounds. For these students, picture cards can help the instructor know whether the student understands the meaning of the words.

Prepare materials
- Make two matching flashcards of the word *at,* printing the word at the left edge of the flashcard so it will match up with a consonant (as if the first letter had been cut off).
- Make flashcards with the letters *f, c, b, s, r, m,* and *h* that are printed on the right edge of the flashcard so they will match up with the *at* flashcards to make a word.

Demonstrate changing the initial consonant to create different words
- Requires three choices of letters (*b, c* and *m*) and family word (*at*).
- One at a time, place each letter side-by-side with the family word. For example, place the letter *c* next to (on the left side of) *at,* saying, "I'm making a word. What word did I make?"
- Provide feedback: "Yes! It says *cat*!" emphasizing sound *k* and sound *at* separately, then blending sounds to form *cat*: "*k-at, cat."* For incorrect responses, ask the student to repeat the word and direct him to look it up on the picture card.
- Repeat the procedure with the other letters (*b* and *m*).

Student changes initial consonant to make words
- Tell the student it is his turn to make a word.
- Direct the student to select a letter and place it with *at* (immediately at the left).
- If he does not read the word he has created spontaneously, ask him to read it.
- Provide feedback: "Yes! It says *bat*!", emphasizing the *b* sound. Refer the student to the picture card if necessary.
- Have the student make and say two more words by changing the first letter.

Student makes words on verbal cue

In response to verbal direction, the student selects the correct consonant and pairs it with the family word to make the word.

- Give the verbal cue: "Make *bat,*" emphasizing the sound of the first letter.
- Provide feedback as the student selects the correct letter and makes the word: "You did it correctly! You made *bat*!" If the student makes an error, point out the difference and simply ask him to try again.
- Guide the student to change the letters, taking away the consonant of the previous word and replacing it with a different consonant to form a new word.
- Repeat until the student correctly spells out all three words.

Student selects letters on "name of letter" cue and makes words

- Verbally cue the student to select a particular letter and pair it with a family word to form a word: "Take the *m*, put it with *at*."
- The student takes the letter (or is guided to do so), makes the word, and is asked to say or sign the word.
- Provide feedback.
- Repeat the process. The student selects the letters *c* and *b* on verbal cue and makes the words *cat* and *bat*.

Student selects letters on "sound-of-letter" cue and makes words:

- Give the cue: "Take the letter that makes the sound *b*, put it with *at*."
- Once the student correctly makes the word, ask him to read it.
- Provide positive feedback or correct the student as necessary.
- Repeat the process, having the student select *m* and *c* by the sounds they make, and make the words *mat* and *cat*.

Continue this exercise, adding one letter at a time

- When the first three words and letter sounds are mastered, add the other letters in the same word family, one at a time.

Teach the student to spell the words in the word family

Working with word families provides a wonderful opportunity for involving students in the spelling process. By simply teaching students to spell *at*, and then asking them to add the initial consonants to make words in the family grouping, students will be able to spell many words in a very short period of time. If a student is unable to print, or prints very slowly, cutout letters can be used, or the child can be asked to input words on the computer. After the student has grasped the skill of spelling within the selected word families, he can use his new words to create sentences either by hand or using a keyboard.

Learning more word families

The preceding activities are designed to show students how phonics works to form words. After children understand this concept, it is not necessary to go through all the steps described above when teaching additional word families. Adapt the techniques to the student's ability to transfer the concept to other word families.

Discriminating word families

As new families are introduced, it is important for the student to be able to discriminate between them. When students have not had an opportunity to practice word families sufficiently, they have a tendency to attend to the first letter only and often assume that the family word is *at,* or the first family word they learned with the initial letter. When the second word family has been introduced, show the student how changing the word family also changes the word.

Discrimination tasks

One consonant, two family words:

For this activity, place one initial consonant flashcard on the student's right left, and the cars of two word families on his right side, as shown below:

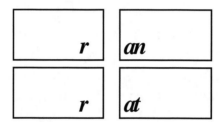

Ask the student to take *an* and put it with the *r* and ask him to read the word (*ran*); repeat with *at* to create the word *rat.*
   • Ask the student to select the family word that goes with *r* to make *ran*, then *rat.*
   • Continue with each consonant that the two families have in common, i.e., *c, f, r, m, v, P,* and *N.*

Two consonants, two family words:

Place two consonants on the left, two family words on the right and ask the student to make specific words, e.g., *fat* and *ran.*

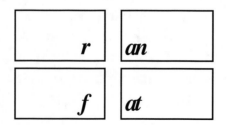

- Cue the student to identify the family word first: "What family is *fat* in? What letter does it start with?" It may be easier for the student to point in response.
- Next, cue the student to first find the letter it starts with, then the family.

Add more consonants:
- Giving more choices, ask the student to find the first letter, then the family.
- Add additional word families as they are introduced.
- If the student makes mistakes in selecting the correct family, have him match, select, and name the family words to review.

Word family books
It is important for students to use word family words in sentences.
- Create language experience books that relate to the student:
    ○ Fluffy is my *cat*. She is a *big, fat cat.*
    ○ Mom hid my *hat.* She *sat* on it.
    ○ Dad hid my *hat* under the *mat.*
- Use word family reading books from other reading programs.
- Use children's literature, such as *The Cat in the Hat,* and other Dr. Seuss books.

Reading word family books
- Start by reading the book to the student, pointing to the word family words, and letting him read some of them. After this has been modeled, allow the student to find and read all of the family words.
- Teach the student to read any words in the story that he does not know as sight words.
- The student works towards reading the book independently.

Choosing new word families for the student
After the student has learned three of the most common word families (*at*, *an* and *et*) and understands the concept of how the word family system works, introduce new families based on words he already knows, words that he has a use for, and words that relate to his interests. Examples:
- If he is reading the word *dog* (as in "Max is my *dog*"), teach him the *og* family.
- If he is reading *boy* (as in "I *am* a *boy*"), teach him the *am* and *oy* families
    ○ The Dr. Seuss book, *Green Eggs and Ham* is especially helpful in teaching the *am* family.

The Word Families

Consonant, Vowel, Consonant (CVC)
- *ag:* bag, rag, sag, tag, wag;
- *an:* ban, can, fan, man, pan, ran, tan, van;

- *ap:* cap, map, gap, nap, rap, lap, sap, zap;
- *at:* bat, cat, fat, hat, mat, rat, sat;
- *en:* den, hen, men, pen, ten;
- *ed:* bed, fed, led, red, wed;
- *et:* bet, get, jet, let, met, net, pet, set, vet, wet, yet;
- *od:* cod, nod, pod;
- *ob:* job, mob, rob, sob;
- *op:* cop, hop, mop, pop, top;
- *ot:* cot, dot, got, hot, lot;
- *oy:* boy, joy, soy, toy;
- *it:* bit, fit, kit, pit, sit, wit;
- *in:* bin, fin, pin, tin, win;
- *im:* dim, him, rim;
- *id:* bid, did, lid, mid, rid;
- *ig:* big, dig, fig, jig, pig, rig, wig;
- *un:* bun, fun, gun, nun, run, sun;
- *um:* gum, hum, sum.

Diagraphs and Consonant Blends with Word Families

In the English language, single letters represent certain sounds, and letter combinations represent other sounds. Letter combinations appearing in the initial position of words are called digraphs and consonant blends.
- **Digraphs:** ch, sh, th, wh
- **Consonant blends:** bl, cr, fr, pl, sc, sl, sp, st, thr, br, dr, gl, pr, scr, sm, spr, str, tr, cl, fl, gr, qu, sk, sn, squ, sw, tw

Use the same method to teach digraphs and consonant blends paired with family words as used for teaching words formed with single letters.
- Add digraph and consonant blend pages to the student's personalized alphabet book.
  o Make a page featuring each digraph and consonant blend as it is introduced.
- Make and play lotto games.
- Play Sound Basketball and Sound Bowling.
- Put the words in sentences and books.

Words created by combining digraphs and consonant blends with word families
- *ag:* stag, brag, drag, flag, snag;
- *am:* clam, cram, gram, swam;
- *an:* clan, plan, bran, scan, span, than;
- *at:* flat, slat, swat, scat, that;
- *ap:* clap, flap, trap, wrap, snap, chap;
- *ed:* bled, fled, sled, sped, shed;

- *en:* then, when;
- *id:* slid, grid, skid;
- *im:* slim, brim, grim, prim, trim, swim, skim, whim;
- *in:* grin, twin, skin, spin, chin, shin, thin;
- *it:* slit, grit, spit, split;
- *op:* stop, chop, shop;
- *og:* clog, frog, smog;
- *ot:* blot, clot, plot, trot, spot, shot;
- *ob:* blob, sob, glob;
- *un:* spun, stun, shun;
- *ug:* slug, snug, chug;
- *ut:* shut, rut, nut;
- *um:* plum, sum, drum, gum.

Three-Letter Word Families
- *ame:* came, dame, frame, game, tame, name, same, flame, blame, shame;
- *ain:* gain, pain, rain, plain, slain, drain, train, strain, grain, Spain, stain, chain;
- *ock:* sock, dock, rock, jock, lock, block, clock, flock, smock, stock, shock;
- *ook:* book, cook, look, hook, nook, took, brook, shook;
- *amp:* camp, damp, lamp, ramp, clamp, cramp, champ;
- *are:* care, bare, dare, fare, rare, flare, scare, stare, share;
- *oat:* goat, coat, boat, moat, float;
- *ing:* ding, ping, ring, sing, wing, bring, swing, sting, thing.

Stage 2: Practice to Fluency
The following activities make practice and review interesting and fun:
Slide-Through Games:

Make slide-through games using tag board and, when possible, laminate.
- **Initial Consonants Slide:** Students slide consonants through the slits, making words and practicing reading and saying the sounds.

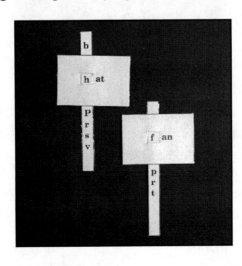

- **Digraphs and Consonant Blends Slide:** Students slide the digraphs and consonant blends through the slits, making words and practicing reading and saying the sounds.
- **Family Words Slide:** Students slide the family words through the slits and read the words, practicing the initial sound and discriminating the word families.

Word Family Wheel Game:
- Students turn the wheel, making words, reading them, and opening the flap for feedback. (See Appendix for T11.1., T11.2., T11.3., T11.4. reproducible word family wheels).

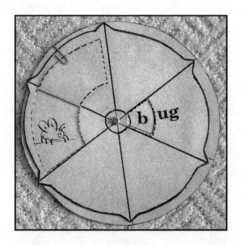

Lotto Games:
- **Picture to Word**
  - Each lotto card has a word family word printed on it (See Appendix T11.5. for reproducible lotto card).
  - Using milk jug caps, make disks with pictures (line drawings) that corresponds to the lotto cards (See Appendix T11.6. for reproducible lotto cards).
  - Students practice comprehension by matching the picture to the word.

• **Picture to Word Family**

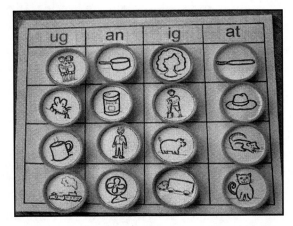

  o Use lotto card with columns and print word families at the top of each column: *at, ug, ig, an* (See Appendix for T11.7. reproducible lotto card).
  ‣ Student practices saying the words, determining to which word family they belong, and places the pictures in the correct column.

• **Word to Word Family**

  o Use lotto card with columns and print a word family name at the top of each column (picture to word family card).
  o Playing cards have words from the families printed on them.
  o Student practices reading the words and discriminating word families.

Word Family Basketball:
• Tape labels of word family names to baskets, waste baskets, buckets, or available containers, starting with the first two word families introduced, and add a basket for each new family introduced (up to four baskets).
• Students toss bean bags into baskets, taking turns if more than one player.
• Students score: one point is earned for making a basket, one point for naming the word family, one point for saying a word that belongs to the word family.

Word Family Bowling:
• Tape labels of word family names to large plastic bottles. If necessary, put some water or sand in them so that they are not tipsy.
• Students toss balls or bean bags to knock over the bottles.
• Students score one point for knocking over a bottle, one point for naming the word family, one point for saying a word in that family.

Word Family Book:
• Students make books featuring a word family on each page.
• Students find pictures of objects in each word family, cut them out, and paste them on the appropriate page.
• If a student is verbal, he can practice saying the words, emphasizing the initial consonant. If a student is non-verbal, he can practice making the appropriate hand sign.

Stage 3: Transfer
Reading Word Family Words with Different Presentations
The student will work towards being able to read word families presented in different fonts, different sizes, different colors, on different color paper, on different surfaces, and in different contexts.

Stage 4: Generalization
Reading Word Family Words Anywhere, Anytime, in Any Presentation
The student has embedded family words and letter sounds in his long-term memory and is able to recognize them in any format and in any context.

Word Sorting
Word sorting is an analogy-based phonics instruction technique that encourages students to study words by examining similarities and differences among spelling and sound patterns (Joseph and McCachran, 2003). This activity is a good follow-up to word families and emphasizes both the visual and auditory components of words.

The student receives a shuffled stack of cards with word family category words printed on them, and sorts the cards visually according to the spelling and/or letter patterns of the category words. Alternatively, to address auditory learning, the teacher or a peer "calls" the word verbally and the student decides to which sound group or word family the word belongs. This is an excellent review and reinforcement activity for all students.

Directions for word-sorting exercise:
• Label each of three margarine tubs with word families *at, an,* and *og.*

- Using a stack of shuffled cards featuring words from the word families, the teacher or caller reads each word and the student takes the card and places it in the appropriate tub. The sound of the word called matches the letters indicated on the tub.
- This is an excellent game for practicing turn-taking and for reinforcing both phonemic awareness and spelling skills.

Summary:

Developing recognition of word families and understanding that combining letters in certain ways results in different word sounds and different meanings are important as they help students build word attack/decoding skills. Working with word families forces students to attend to the "insides" of words, rather than making guesses based on initial consonant sounds. Working with word families also encourages students to develop an understanding of transfer: as a syllable has a particular sound in one word, so it will in another. Students work toward being able to transfer "chunks" of sounds from one word to another, thus improving both the speed and accuracy of word recognition.

12

CHAPTER TWELVE:
SPELLING

Being able to spell is an important skill for all learners, including those who have special learning needs. Some students will be able to participate in traditional spelling programs, while others will require a more specialized approach. Students may need adaptations for practice and testing, and the rate at which new words are presented may need to be reduced. The success of the student, as always, is the prime consideration.

When and Where to Start

Once students are able to match, select, and name all the letters in the words on their spelling lists, they are ready to start spelling. The best first word to teach is usually the student's name, provided it is a simple name to spell (has six or less letters), or can be shortened (Christopher to Chris, Suzanne to Sue). This should be a consideration when the student is learning to read and is expected to say his name.

Teaching students to spell *Mom, Dad*, or a special interest word, is another option for first words. The important factor in selecting words is to choose a word for which the student has a use and/or is based on a topic of interest. Teach the student to spell the words in several of the common word families, such as *at, an, it* and *og*. As other word families are added to the student's list, the number of words he will be able to spell will increase greatly.

The spelling of words can be communicated in one of two ways: orally stating letters in order, spelling bee style, "Daddy, D-a-d-d-y, Daddy;" or writing the word on any surface using any writing equipment, including paper and pencil, letter tiles, cut-out plastic letters, magnet letters, letter flashcards or a keyboard and word processing program.

Strategies for Teaching Spelling:

The Student's Name
• Matching letters:

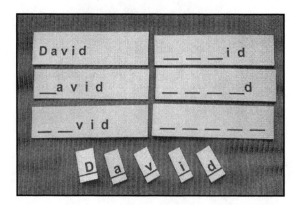

- ○ Spell the student's name, pointing at each letter as you go along, and say the name, e.g., "D-a-v-i-d spells *David*," to explain what spelling is.
- ○ Have the student practice matching plastic or foam letters under the letters of his name using an elimination technique. Initially, place most of the plastic letters under the sample, gradually decreasing until he is able to put them all in order.
- ○ Fill in the blanks: Place several of the letters in order and see if the student can fill in the blanks. Again, using an elimination technique, increase the number of blanks until the student can select all the letters of his name in order, independently.
- ○ When all the letters are in order, ask the student to spell his name aloud as he points to each letter. Reinforce by saying, "You spelled David!"
- ○ If the student makes a mistake, model the correct response and ask him to try again.
- ○ When the student is able to print, start with a "fill in the blanks" process, gradually increasing the number of letters for the student to fill in.

Encourage students to practice often by printing their names on their artwork, picture journals, and worksheets. Additionally (or alternately if the student is unable to print), encourage students to input their names on the computer, selecting the correct keys in order, working from a sample if necessary.

Additional Spelling Techniques

The previously mentioned method is designed for students who need carefully programmed steps to learn to spell their names. As they mature and need to know the spelling of other words, some students will continue to need this careful programming. For these students, spelling words should be selected carefully, according to the frequency with which they are needed.

Some students will be able to learn to spell using traditional spelling techniques, and some will require modifications. One method is to direct students to look up the correct spelling in their word banks, personal dictionaries, or word books (such as the book, *The First Word Book Ever* by Richard Scarry, which has pictures and words organized by category). Regardless of the method used, take the opportunity to emphasize the letter sounds and cue students to use these sounds when spelling.

Copy-Cover-Write-Compare-Correct

The copy-cover-write-compare-correct method is the most common method used to teach spelling. The student learns to spell by being directed through the following steps:
- Looking at the word and studying it,
- Covering up the word,
- Writing it,
- Comparing the word he has written to the model,
- Correcting errors,
- Repeating the process until proficiency is reached.

Weekly Spelling Lists

The weekly list is a traditional approach to spelling. Each week students may work either on the classroom spelling list, a modified list, or a list of words derived from their personal vocabularies. Words are generally learned through a memorization or rote learning process of daily practice in printing or keyboarding the words, rehearsing their spelling, using the words in sentences, and, finally, participating in a weekly spelling test. When testing, allow students to reply orally, by signing, by print, or by using a keyboard—whatever method will allow them to be most successful.

Tape-recorded Lessons

Using a tape recorder to record a lesson can free up teacher time and allows students to work independently at their own level and learning rate. Students working with tape-recorded lessons use earphones and practices spelling by writing, selecting, and arranging movable letters, or by using a keyboard. Recording an actual lesson with the student will assure that the pace matches his ability level. Taped lessons can be repeated as necessary. An example of a tape:
- *Break, b-r-e-a-k, break* (spelled so student can hear the flow of the letters).
- Now you spell it, *b—r—e—a—k* (pauses between letters give student enough time to write, or select and arrange each letter, or find it and key it into the computer).
- Check your work, *b-r-e-a-k*?
- Cover your work and write it by yourself—*break.*
- Check your work, *b-r-e-a-k.*

Limit the number of practice words to about five. When these have been mastered, begin a new list. Periodically, review and reinforce previously learned words.

Computer Spelling Programs

Computer programs provide practice in drill, unscrambling letters, filling in the missing letters, and using words in sentences. Select programs that allow the instructor to select the words, and make certain the program matches the student's ability level. Remember that computer programs provide practice, transfer, and generalization, but do not take the place of providing instruction and an ongoing opportunity for students to spell, write, and use the words.

Summary:

For many students, the development of spelling skills is a gradual process that depends upon an awareness of sound/symbol associations, knowledge of word families, and the acuity of their visual and auditory memories. Learning to spell is also a process of rote memorization. Ongoing practice in spelling words (orally, by printing, or by keyboarding) will be beneficial to students as they participate in other writing tasks, such as composition. For students who have special learning needs, it is important to praise all efforts, allowing them to develop confidence in their ability to engage in the writing process.

13

CHAPTER THIRTEEN:
INCLUSION IN THE SCHOOL CURRICULUM

One of the greatest benefits of the strength-based approach to literacy presented in this book is that it can be applied to any subject. Its use is not restricted to language or reading classes. The methodology is "portable" and can be used to teach vocabulary in any subject area, such as social studies or science. Participation in literacy instruction is not contingent upon the mastery of the traditional set of sub-skills; rather, students are able to participate immediately with varying degrees of support and modification.

As instruction in a thematic unit begins, the student participates in learning new theme-based vocabulary. Words may be learned during a language arts period or during the actual subject time. Instructors teaching new theme-based vocabulary should:
- Introduce new words before lessons to prepare students to receive new information and enhance their ability to comprehend lessons;
- Review and reinforce thematic vocabulary on a regular basis;
- Add theme words to students' personal dictionaries;
- Add flashcards of theme words to the students' word banks;
- Include theme words on spelling lists, word searches and other review activities.

The Planning and Evaluation Chart (See Appendix for T13.1. Planning and Evaluation Chart) provides assistance in planning how students will participate in lessons and thematic units across all subject areas.

Strategies for Inclusion in Subject-specific Thematic Units
Vocabulary Instruction
- Choose key vocabulary for the thematic unit and teach using the match, select, and name method.

- Provide student with notebooks in which subject-specific words can be listed. It may also be useful to create flashcards for students to use for sentence construction or to indicate answers for subject-related questions.
- Have students construct sentences using the subject-specific vocabulary words. The sentences can be about pictures, video presentations and information or pictures that they have gathered from books or downloaded from the internet.
- Instruct students to copy sentences into a notebook to accompany illustrations or type them into a word processing program, then cut them out and paste them onto the appropriate page.
- Have students practice reading information that has been modified for their ability level. Content may be abbreviated or language may be simplified so that only key concepts are dealt with.

Scrapbooks & Binders

Preparing scrapbooks or binders by gathering and presenting information about a particular subject area in a visual format is an excellent way for students with special learning needs to participate in the curriculum. Scrapbooks may include the following items:
- Worksheets;
- Coloring pages, diagrams, maps, etc.;
- Illustrations from magazines and other sources;
- Photographs of the subject matter;
- Photographs of the student engaging in work on the topic as well as participating in group work with classmates;
- Subject-specific word grids and flashcards (in a plastic pocket, freezer bag or page protector);
- All of the student's writing (either printing or keyboarding) on the topic;
- Copies of particular passages that the student has been reading for information and practice.

The scrapbook shown below was created in conjunction with a lesson about the home. It includes pictures of items found in each room of a typical home. Catalogues and magazines were used as sources for the illustrations, and photographs of various rooms in the student's home were also included.

Theme Books

Theme books that address a specific aspect of a thematic unit are useful learning tools. The student whose book appears in the example below participated in a unit on life cycles, specifically studying the life cycle of the beetle and learning the associated vocabulary. She participated in all the classroom lessons, and at the end of the unit, read her book about mealworms and beetles to the class.

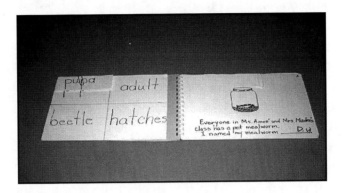

For students with special learning needs in mainstreamed classrooms, this methodology enables meaningful academic inclusion by allowing them to be perceived as learners by others, a crucial aspect of successful inclusion. Furthermore, it allows visual learners to access a broader body of knowledge. Themes addressed may include the community, nature, foods, clothing, dressing, holidays and traditions.

Individualized binders, books, or scrapbooks, provide immediate access to word recognition, serve as practical visual formats for gathering information, and provide an entertaining and well-organized means to facilitate student participation in learning. Throughout the school year, these books become "souvenirs" that can be reviewed and revisited, thus reinforcing previously taught material.

Mathematics

While mathematics primarily concerns the world of numbers, spatial concepts and data management, it is also a subject area that is heavily imbued with language. By applying the match, select, and name method, students can easily learn the vocabulary of mathematics.

Language-related goals:
- Learning to read number words.
- Knowing the names of the operations.
- Being able to read and follow operational instructions independently.
- Being able to read word problems.
- Discerning the operations required in word problems, taking cues from the language of the problem.

- Being able to talk about numbers, operations and the components of word problems.
- Being able to read the time of day in word as well as numeric form.

Creating a Dictionary for the Vocabulary of Mathematics

Include all vocabulary that the student will need to know in a math dictionary. Words may include the names of the operations, number words, time words, instructional words and phrases (such as *draw a line*, *using a ruler*, etc.). This book should be added to on a regular basis and should move with the student as he progresses through school. Words should be organized by mathematical strand: number sense and numeration, algebra and patterning, geometry and spatial sense, data management and probability and measurement. It is useful to show an example of the math concept along with the vocabulary word. If this approach is being used, a binder is a useful format.

Word Problems

The ability to solve mathematical word problems is dependent upon the ability to read. The student must be able to understand the language of the problem and this can present a formidable challenge for many students with special learning needs. The following steps can be used:

- Directly pre-teach the language of the problems: how many, how much, etc.;
- Assist the student in locating key words and phrases;
- When possible or necessary, provide a visual model of the elements of the problem, such as, how many apples, the length and width of the room, etc.;
- It may be necessary to first read problems to students and then help them read problems independently. For many students, repeated readings will be necessary until basic problem formats are recognized and the expected operations and steps are discerned.

Time

The language of time can be very abstract for many students with special needs. It is important not only to teach students to read these words, but also to make an effort to use the vocabulary of time so that they become familiar with the concepts.

Key vocabulary and concepts include:
- *yesterday, today, tomorrow;*
- *past, present, future;*
- *now, later;*
- *then, long ago;*
- *minute, hour;*
- *day, week, month, etc.;*
- *last week, next week, etc.;*
- *in awhile, in a minute;*
- *soon.*

Participation in traditional classroom calendar activities can be useful, but dates and the concepts of yesterday, today and tomorrow should be reviewed individually with students using their own calendars. This will help them develop an understanding of temporal concepts, and may also transfer to understanding sequence in reading comprehension and creative writing.

The use of a visual schedule is a key component of the learning program for many students with special learning needs. As students acquire more and more vocabulary, it will be important for them to learn to read the subject names, as well as to tell time. Ideally, students will move from a picture or symbol-based schedule system to a schedule comprised of subject and event names, along with the digital representations of time. Local television schedules are excellent tools for making time concepts meaningful to the student. Learning to read and locate the names (a well as the times) of favorite television programs is an important life skill and can be an element of the student's reading program at school or a reinforcement activity at home.

The Planning and Evaluation Chart: Across the Curriculum

The planning and evaluation chart provides instructors with a useful tool for both planning instruction for and evaluating individual students. The chart (See Appendix for T13.1.) prompts the instructor to take the following steps:
- Outline all of the elements that the student will be expected to learn, such as key vocabulary and concepts.
- List all materials that may be useful to include in instruction, such as books, videos, magazines, photographs, art materials, diagrams, etc.
- State the expectations for the student's final presentation or project—what kind of work will be required for the purpose of evaluation?
- Identify the desired outcome: What should the student take away from this learning experience?
- In evaluating a student, note the following on the chart:
  - What art work has he produced?
  - What vocabulary has he learned?
  - Can he indicate understanding of the concept, either verbally or non-verbally (through pointing, fill in the blanks, exercises, etc.)?
  - Did the student make any presentation to the class? How did that go?
  - What level of assistance did the student receive? Did the student work in a group?

Utilizing this simple chart provides an excellent means for collecting data for report cards and individual education plans.

Summary:

The match, select, and name approach to whole word sight recognition allows students to easily acquire theme-specific words, enabling them to participate in the literacy aspects of school curriculum across all subject areas. By being able to recognize theme words in print and say (or sign) them, students are better able to comprehend classroom lessons, because they are better able to receive information, having been prepared to recognize words both visually and auditorily. The use of scrapbooks and binders further improve the likelihood of successfully including students with disabilities in the regular curriculum by providing useful formats for collecting and storing subject-specific information. They also act as effective tools for organizing information and print material, and as good visual aids to help students with review and recall of information.

14

CHAPTER FOURTEEN:
OVERVIEW OF SKILL DEVELOPMENT IN LITERACY

This book was written to provide educators with a methodological approach for teaching literacy skills to students with special learning needs, including students with Autism Spectrum Disorder and Down syndrome, who have difficulty learning to read through a traditional auditory, sound-based approach. While phonemic decoding skills may eventually develop for these students, they are not readily acquired. This approach to literacy skill development offers teachers an alternative that focuses on visual learning, which is the preferred learning modality for most special needs students with ADS and DS.

Whole word sight recognition is the foundation skill for this method. A sight vocabulary is built based initially on words that are personally relevant and meaningful to the student. Students are easily and quickly engaged in reading words in sentences. Flashcards are used in the initial stage so as to bypass the physical process of writing or keyboarding, thus allowing students' cognitive energy to be focused on making meaningful statements with the printed word.

The four stages of learning—acquisition, practice to fluency, skill transfer and generalization—are the basis for this approach and have been outlined in detail so that no stage is neglected or forgotten as the student progresses. The key component of the acquisition stage is the match, select, and name method which engages the four learning styles: visual, auditory, kinesthetic and digital. Success at the acquisition stage is critical and this simple approach allows students who have special learning needs to be successful.

As a logical sequitur to learning to read and create sentences, students are actively engaged in reading books, initially about themselves, their environment, and their special interests, but working towards books based on curriculum content and classroom work.

While students may or may not be able to read at grade level, they will nevertheless be able to actively participate in literacy and learn about their world from print.

Reading must also become a source of pleasure for these students, who acquire the skill less easily than their typical peers. It is incumbent upon parents and teachers to make the process enjoyable so that the student perceives its worth. Reading is a skill that can lead to enjoyment throughout students' lives, and influence their potential for future employment.

Starting with the simple act of creating sentences with flashcards, students are taken through the steps of learning to convey thoughts with words and to commit them to paper or a word processing program. Looking to the future and the use of electronic communication devices, learning to spell and compose words will be an essential skill.

Overview of Implementation

The following list of steps is intended to provide the teacher with clear guidelines for teaching literacy skills. It is meant to be a quick reference for use when actively engaged in the process. Teachers may discover new or extra steps for their particular student(s); incorporating individualized features only adds to the richness of the experience.

Seeing these steps listed also allows teachers to quickly discern where their students are in the process: perhaps they already have matching skills and know the alphabet; perhaps they can already read some words, but are struggling as expectations become more complex and a faster rate of learning is required.

The overview also allows parents and caregivers to see "at a glance" what their child is experiencing in the process of learning to read. These steps may also be used to develop the student's Individual Education Plan as they provide a guideline for progression and offer prescribed next steps when necessary.

OVERVIEW:
1) Develop matching skills: while the development of matching skills can involve very sophisticated processes, the following steps provide a useful and basic skill-building sequence:
    a) Shape to Shape: Many young students with ASD have difficulty with matching objects because they may become distracted by their attributes and lose sight of the objective of the task. Matching simple, two-dimensional black shapes is an easy starting point. At the beginning of the process, it is important to reduce the variables so that students can discern to the goal of the activity.

 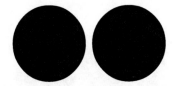

b) Object to Object: Three dimensional objects such as blocks or toys are matched with like objects.

c) Picture to Picture: The matching board shown below was made using simple Boardmaker™ (Mayer-Johnson) shapes.

d) Picture to Object: The student matches a picture of an object, such as a rubber ball, to the actual object (symbolic stage).

e) Match word to word under picture: "Test" with the use of the distracter card.

f) Match words to words: Use the match, select, and name process.
   *Words are usually learned in increments of four, although an instructor must make this decision based on the abilities of the student. Some students may initially have more success learning two or three words at a time.

2) Vocabulary is based on personal and meaningful words that represent family members, favorite foods, pets, relatives, friends, toys, cartoon characters, etc.

3) In the initial stages, students match words to pictures to check word recognition and comprehension (this is *comprehension check, not* the learning process). After students have demonstrated that they can successfully match words to pictures for approximately 25 words, a reasonably safe assumption can be made that they understand words familiar to their environment. Nevertheless, ongoing probes are important for assessment, particularly as students move into subject-specific vocabulary across the curriculum.

4) Add sentence builders (e.g., the Dolch word lists) to sight vocabulary. After the first two word grids, add one or two sentence builders to each grid, always accompanying them with at least two higher interest words. Recommended sentence builder starter words include: *like, and, the, here, is, my, a, go, to, in, eat, play, with*.

5) Students create sentences with vocabulary words. Use a sentence board to create sentences, then have students copy sentences with a duplicate set of flashcards.

6) Work towards extending sentence length: *I see Mommy; I see Mommy and Daddy; I see Mommy and Daddy in the house.*

7) Work towards having students create sentences independently.

8) Create two or more personal books for each student, making sure they have been taught all the words that appear. The child should be able to read the books completely independently—to a wide and appreciative audience!

9) When students have learned approximately 25-50 words, create a personal dictionary and begin to incorporate phonics. It is important for students to learn letters in a context: i.e., *M* is for *Mommy, D* is for *Daddy, D* is for *David*, etc.

10) As new words are learned, add them to students' personal dictionaries and underline the initial consonant. Also, underline or highlight familiar syllables, such as *tion* or *ter*.

11) Create an alphabet scrapbook with a page for each letter. Include pictures of things that start with each letter for regular review, stressing initial consonant sounds.

12) When students are able to recognize 30 to 50 words, introduce word families, starting with the *at* family. At this time, also engage students in word sorting activities in which they physically sort words according to their spelling, both visually and auditorily (by how they look or by how they sound).

13) Begin teaching spelling skills for the most familiar words. This may require the use of memorization, initial sound cues, and daily practice in printing/typing spelling words. The extent to which this activity can be applied will depend significantly on the child's fine motor or keyboard abilities.

14) Choose a print book based on the student's interests, and *teach to the book*. Conduct an analysis of the words that the child does not know and methodically teach each word, using the match, select, and name method. Continue until the child can read the book independently.

15) As students' sight vocabularies grow, keep words on word rings (typically purchased at stationary stores in the binder section) or in specially created word banks for regular review. Review is essential until the words are thoroughly generalized and consolidated in memory.

16) Continue to expand vocabulary, introducing vocabulary from other subject areas.

17) Review, review, review: use games; make new and longer sentences; use the child's interests, favorite TV shows, movies, pets, friends, etc. for subject matter, making reading meaningful. The child should be invested in the process.

18) Continue to teach the child to read more books. As time goes on, fewer words will need to be taught because the child's sight vocabulary will increase substantially, as will as his ability to decode new words.

19) As the child becomes more and more comfortable with the reading process, work towards and focus on the development of comprehension skills.

20) Keep in mind that reading and spelling are two very different processes. The student may be able to participate in the classroom spelling program, although modifications may be necessary. To the extent possible, the words that the student learns to spell should also be words that he can read and use in sentences. Isolated words that have no context will not be useful and there is less likelihood that they

will be retained. Part of a student's modified spelling program can be based on his personal vocabulary words.

21) Continue to work on sentence building activities with the student. Sentence creation is crucial to the thinking and writing processes. Sentence building naturally extends to participation in journal writing activities and story creation and needs to be a segment of each day's literacy experience.

22) In parallel fashion, the student needs to work on the physical aspects of creating print. For many students, the most efficient writing tool will be a keyboard. Difficulty with the motor planning aspects of printing and handwriting may hinder the thinking process and prevent the student from being able to do his best work. The goal is for the student to commit ideas in symbolic form (words) to paper (or a screen); the tool that he uses to accomplish this is irrelevant.

23) As the student's skills grow, literacy skills need to extend to materials in the environment beyond the school, including restaurants, catalogues and magazines.

24) As the student progresses, he will continue to develop word attack and decoding skills; however, from time to time it may be necessary to go back to the original match, select, and name strategy when a new and particularly challenging word comes along. Use of this familiar, secure, and comforting routine may enable the student to get through a temporary impasse.

From time to time, a student may balk at participating in literacy activities (or other subject areas). If this happens, consider the following questions:

1) Is the student bored? Has he reviewed the same words over and over until he no longer wants to participate because it's just more of the same old thing?

2) Does the subject matter have any relevance to the student's experience?

3) Are things moving too slowly? Many students are more successful when lessons move along quickly. While the teacher's first instinct may be to move slowly and carefully, very often students are better able to learn and retain lessons when they are presented with words and put through sentence building activities at a fairly brisk pace. This is particularly true for many students with ASD.

4) Would it be worthwhile to put reading aside for a time? Doing so will not cause any harm and it may be the "pause that refreshes." Upon returning to literacy skill building, start with a new and engaging topic.

Summary:

When working with special needs students, individualization is expected and required. The methodology presented in this book is intended to provide instructors with a detailed plan for taking students through the stages of learning, engaging all students in progressive participation in literacy.

Appendix

T3.1.   Standard Flashcards

These can be copied on to stock paper, usually with a manual feed to a copying machine.

T3.2.   Standard Word Grid

T4.1. Reading Progress Graph

Name: _____ **Task/Game:** _____**Week of:** _____

	Sunday	Monday	Tuesday	Wednesday	Thursday	Friday	Saturday
10							
9							
8							
7							
6							
5							
4							
3							
2							
1							
0							

T4.2. Small Circle Templates

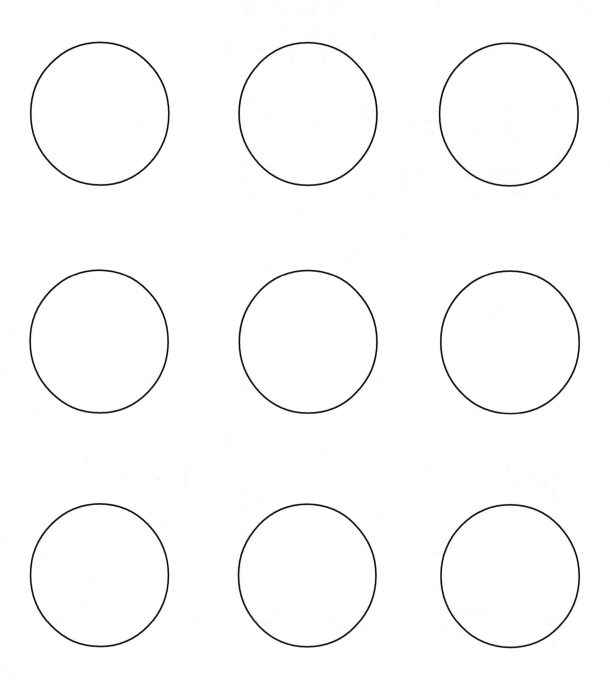

T4.3.　Large Circle Templates

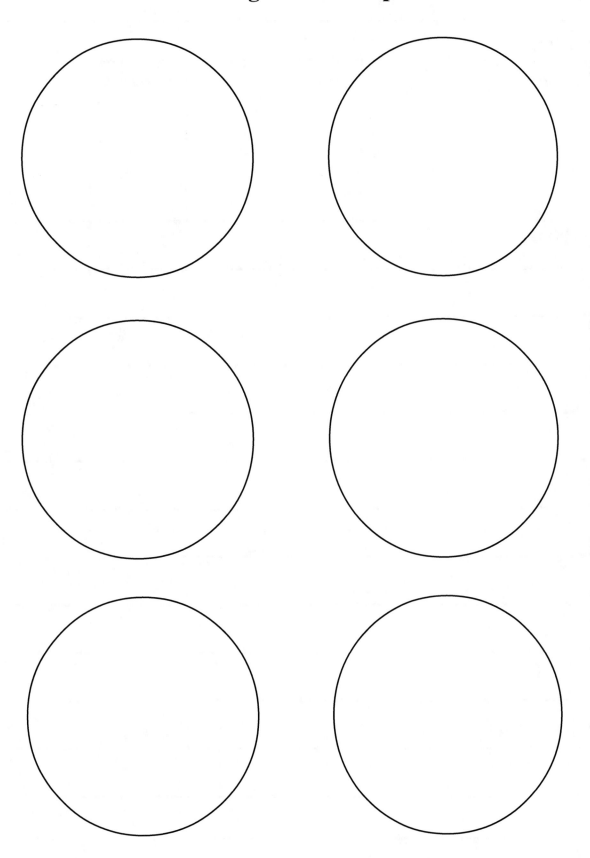

T8.1.　Reading Comprehension Response Chart

Title:		
Who:	**Where?**	**When?**
What?		

T8.2.   Reading Comprehension Response Chart

What happened in the story?
The beginning — how did the story start?
The middle — describe the action:
The end — how did the story finish?

T9.1.   Basic Story Elements

Who:	Where:
When:	**What:**

T9.2.   My Story

Who is the story about?	Where does the story take place?
Who are the other characters in the story?	List some describing words about the location:
When does the action in the story take place?	What will happen in the story? What will the characters do?

T9.3.　Story Sequence Chart

What's going to happen in my story?
1.
2.
3.
4.
5.
6.
7.
8.
9.
10.

T9.4.   Comic Book Format

1.	2.

3.	4.

T11.1a.   UG Word Family Wheel

Photocopy: Cut out wheels T11.1a. and T11.1b. and cut on dotted lines. Place wheel T11.1a. over wheel T11.1b. and attach at axis.

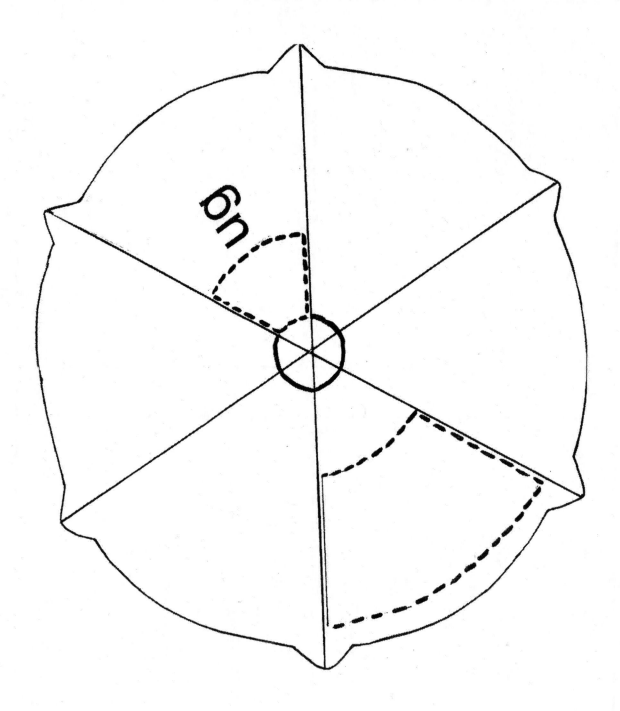

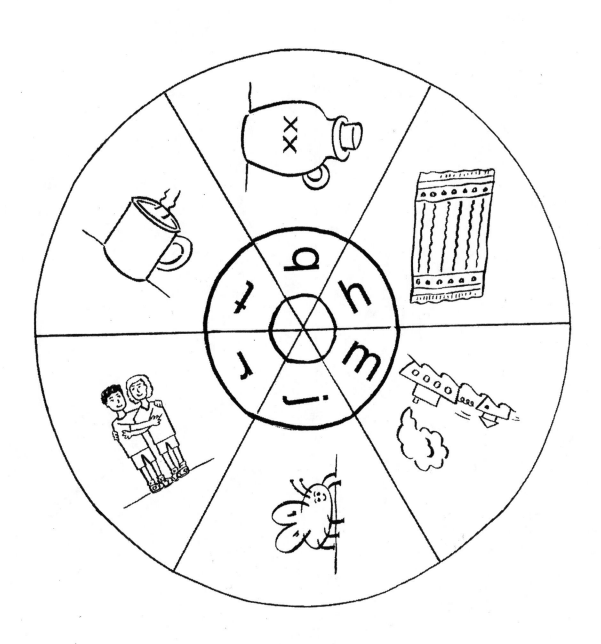

T11.2a.   AN Word Family Wheel

Photocopy: Cut out wheels T11.2a. and T11.2b. and cut on dotted lines. Place wheel T11.2a. over wheel T11.2b. and attach at axis.

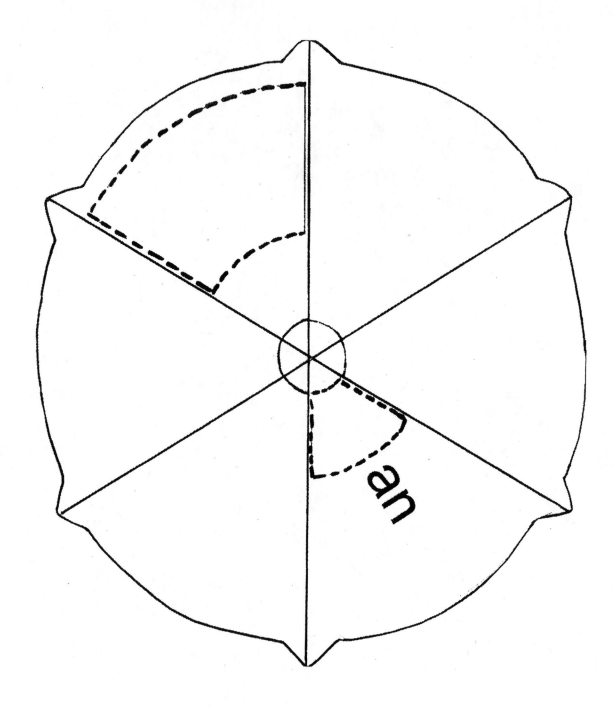

T11.2b.   AN Word Family Wheel

T11.3a.   IG Word Family Wheel

Photocopy: Cut out wheels T11.3a. and T11.3b. and cut on dotted lines. Place wheel T11.3a. over wheel T11.3b. and attach at axis.

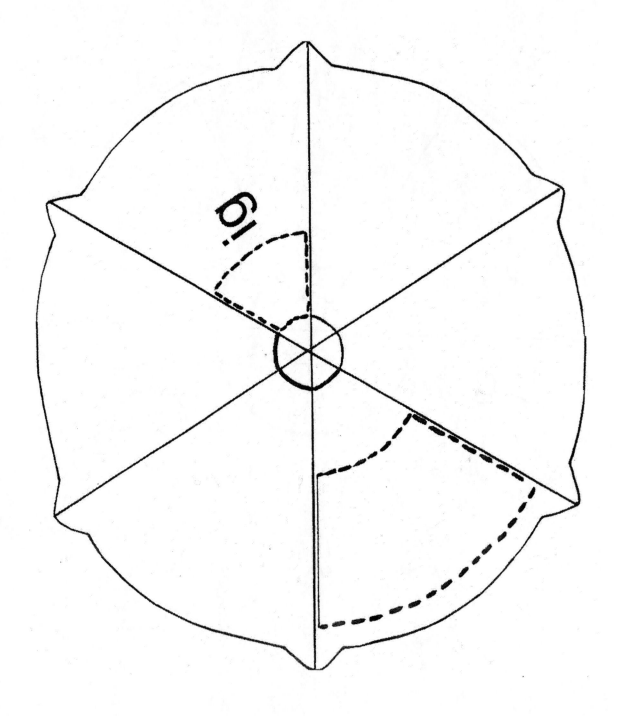

T11.3b.   IG Word Family Wheel

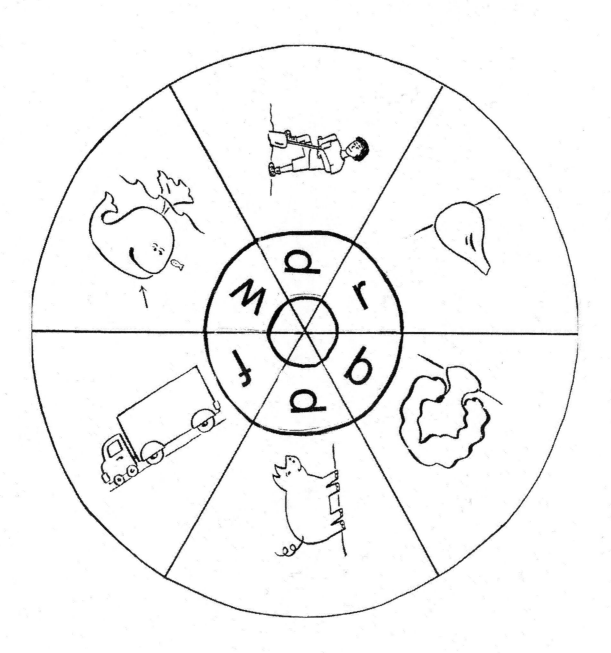

T11.4a. AT Word Family Wheel

Photocopy: Cut out wheels T11.4a. and T11.4b. and cut on dotted lines. Place wheel T11.4a. over wheel T11.4b. and attach at axis.

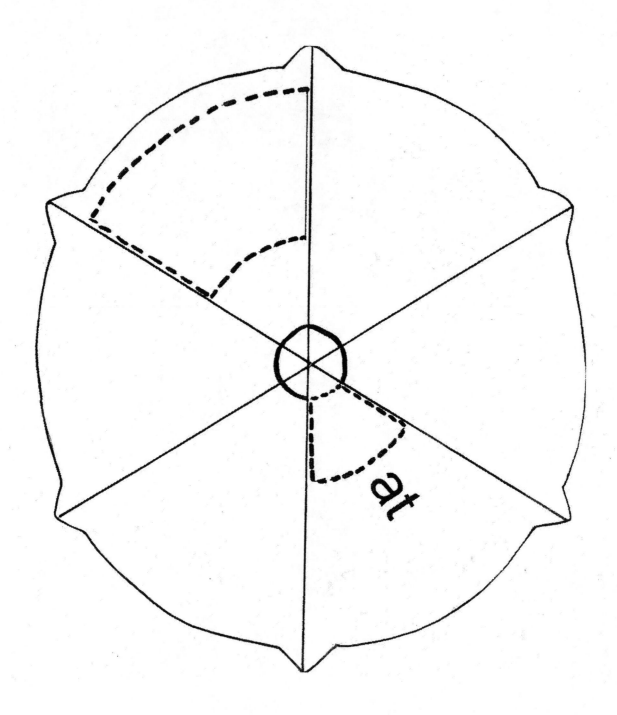

T11.4b. AT Word Family Wheel

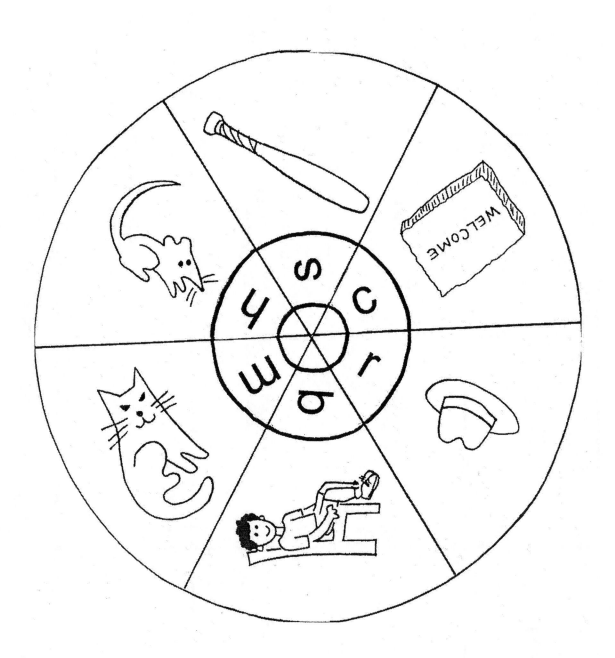

pig	rig	pig	wig
man	fan	pan	can
hat	bat	cat	rat
bug	tug	mug	hug

T11.5. Lotto Word Family Word Cards

T11.7. Word Family Lotto Card

at	ig	an	ug

T13.1. Planning and Evaluation Chart

Student: _____

Subject: _____   **Grade Level:** _____

Unit:
Lesson:
Key Vocabulary:
Key Concepts:
Books/Pictures:
Visual Presentations (videos, DVD's, drama, etc.):
Art Work:
Worksheets:
Writing Activities:
Posters/Collages/Scrapbook:
Participation:
Presentation:
Outcomes:

References

Browder, D.M., Wakeman, S.Y., Spooner, F., Ahlgrim-Delzell, L., & Algozzine, B. (2006). Research on reading instruction for individuals with significant cognitive disabilities. *Exceptional Children, Vol. 72, No. 4*, 392-408.

Council for Exceptional Children. (2005). *Universal design for learning: A guide for teachers and education professionals.* Pearson, Merrill, Prentice Hall.

Fouts, R. (1997). *Next of kin: What chimpanzees have taught me about who we are.* New York, NY: William Morrow and Company, Inc.

Fowler, A.E., Doherty, B.J., Boynton, L. (1995). The basis of reading skills in young adults with Down syndrome. In L. Nadel & D. Rosenthal (Eds.), *Down syndrome: Living and learning in the community,* New York, NY: Wiley-Liss.

Goodman, V. (1995). *Reading is more than phonics!: A parents' guide for reading with beginning or discouraged readers.* Calgary, Alta.: Reading Wings.

Grandin, T. (1995). *Thinking in pictures and other reports from my life with autism.* New York, NY: Doubleday.

Happe, F. (1995). *Autism: an introduction to psychological theory.* Cambridge, MA: Harvard University Press.

Hodgdon, L.A. (1995). *Visual strategies for improving communication: Practical supports for school and home.* Troy, MI: QuirkRoberts Publishing.

Janzen, J.E. (2002). *Understanding the nature of Autism: A practical guide.* San Antonio, TX: Therapy Skill Builders.

Jones, G. (2002). *Educational provision for children with Autism and Asperger Syndrome: Meeting their needs.* London: David Fulton Publishers.

Joseph, L. & McCachran, M. (2003, June). Comparison of a word study phonics technique between students with moderate to mild mental retardation and struggling readers without disabilities. *Education and Training in Developmental Disabilities, Vol. 38, 2.*

Just, M. (2006, June). *Cortical underconnectivity in Autism.* Paper presented at the International Meeting for Autism Research, Montreal, Quebec.

Kliewer, C. (1998). Citizenship in the literate community: An ethnography of children with Down syndrome and the written word. *Exceptional Children. Vol. 64, No. 2*, 176-180.

Kluth, P. (2003). *"You're going to love this kid!" Teaching students with Autism in the inclusive classroom.* Baltimore, MD: Paul H. Brooks Publishing.

Koppenhaver, D.A. et al. (1991, September). The implications of emergent literacy research for children with developmental disabilities. *American Journal of Speech and Language Pathologists,* 38–44.

Koshino, H. et al. (2004). Functional connectivity in an fMRI working memory task in high-functioning Autism. *Neuroimage. Vol. 24, Issue 3*, 810–821.

Mesibov, G. & Howley, M. (2003). *Accessing the curriculum for pupils with Autistic Spectrum Disorders: Using the TEACCH programme to help inclusion.* London: David Fulton Publishers.

Mirenda, P. (2003). "He's not really a reader…": Perspectives on supporting literacy development in individuals with Autism. *Topics in Language Disorders, Vol. 23, No. 4,* 271–282.

Mirenda, P. (2003). Toward functional augmentative and alternative communication for students with Autism: Manual signs, graphic symbols, and voice output communication aids. *Language, Speech and Hearing Services in Schools, Vol. 34,* 203–216.

Oelwein, P.L. (1995). *Teaching reading to children with Down syndrome: A guide for parents and teachers.* Bethesda, MD: Woodbine House Publishing.

Oelwein, P.L. (1999). Individualizing reading for each child's ability and needs. In T.J. Hassold and D. Patterwson (Eds), *Down syndrome: A promising future, together,* 55-64. New York: Wiley-Liss, Inc.

Oelwein, P.L. (2002). Liberation from traditional reading and math teaching methods and measurements. In W.I. Cohen, L. Nadel, and M.E. Madnick (Eds), *Down Syndrome: Visions for the 21st century,* 421-436. New York: Wiley-Liss, Inc.

Quill, K.A. (2000). *Do-watch-listen-say: Social and communication intervention for children with Autism.* Baltimore, MD: Paul H. Brooks Publishing Co.

Scarborough, H.S. & Brady, S.A. (2002). *Education for All: The report of the expert panel on literacy and numeracy instruction for students with special education needs, Kindergarten to Grade 6.* Ontario Ministry of Education, 2005.

Scarborough, H.S. & Brady, S.A. (2002). Toward a common terminology for talking about speech and reading: A glossary of "phon" words and some related terms. *Journal of Literacy Research, 34,* 299-336.

Sundberg, M. & Partington, J. (1998). *Teaching language to children with Autism or other developmental disabilities.* Pleasant Hill, CA: Behavior Analysts, Inc.

Tuchman, R., Daichman, J. & Cueli-Dutil, T. (2002, October). *Motor Deficits in Children with Autism and Related Disorders.* Paper presented at the Geneva Centre Internal Symposium on Autism, Toronto, Ontario, Canada.

Volkmar, F. (1998, October). Expert Panel on Genetics, Geneva Centre Internal Symposium on Autism, Toronto, Ontario, Canada.

Vygotsky, L.S. (1978). *Mind and society: The development of higher mental processes.* Cambridge, MA: Harvard University Press.

Wang, P.P. (1996). A neuropsychological profile of Down syndrome: Cognitive skills and brain morphology. *Mental Retardation and Developmental Disabilities Research Reviews,* 2, 102-108.

Winter, M. (2003). *Asperger Syndrome: What teachers need to know.* London: Jessica Kingsley Publishers, Ltd.

Resources: Print and Video Materials
Available from National Professional Resources, Inc.
1-800 453-7461 • www.NPRinc.com

Allington, Richard L. & Patricia M. Cunningham. (1996). *Schools That Work: Where all Children Read and Write.* New York, NY: Harper Collins.

Allington, Richard. (2005). *What Really Matters for Struggling Readers.* Boston, MA: Allyn & Bacon.

Armstrong, Thomas. (1997). *The Myth of the A.D.D. Child.* New York, NY: Penguin Putnam Inc.

ASCD. (2006). *Teaching Students with Learning Disabilities in the Regular Classroom* (Video). Baltimore, MD: ASDC.

Barnett, D.W., Daly, E.J., Jones, K.M., & Lentz, F.E. (2004). *Response to intervention: Empirically based special service decisions from single-case designs of increasing and decreasing intensity. Journal of Special Education*, 38, 66-79.

Basso, Dianne, & Natalie McCoy. (2002). *The Co-Teaching Manual.* Columbia, SC: Twin Publications.

Bateman, Barbara D. & Annemieke Golly. (2003). *Why Johnny Doesn't Behave: Twenty Tips for Measurable BIPs.* Verona, WI: Attainment Company, Inc.

Bateman, Barbara D. & Cynthia M. Herr. (2003). *Writing Measurable IEP Goals and Objectives.* Verona, WI: Attainment Company, Inc.

Beecher, Margaret. (1995). *Developing the Gifts & Talents of All Students in the Regular Classroom.* Mansfield Center, CT: Creative Learning Press, Inc.

Bender, William. *Differentiating Instruction for Students with Learning Disabilities.* Thousand Oaks, CA: Corwin Press, 2002.

Block, Cathy Collins & Susan Israel. (2005). *Reading First and Beyond.* Thousand Oaks, CA: Corwin Press.

Bray, Marty & Abbie Brown, et al. (2004). *Technology and the Diverse Learner.* Thousand Oaks, CA: Corwin Press.

Brown-Chidsey, Rachel & Mark W. Steege. (2005). *Response to Intervention.* New York, NY: Guilford Press.

Casbarro, Joseph. (2005). *Test Anxiety & What You Can Do About It: A Practical Guide for Teachers, Parents, & Kids.* Port Chester, NY: Dude Publishing.

Chapman, Carolyn & Rita King. (2003). *Differentiated Instructional Strategies for Reading in the Content Areas.* Thousand Oaks, CA: Corwin Press.

Conklin, Wendy. (2006). *Instructional Strategies for Diverse Learners.* Carthage, IL: Shell Publishing.

Copeland, Susan & E. Keefe. (2007). *Effective Literacy Instruction*. Baltimore, MD: Paul H. Brookes Publishing Co.

Council for Exceptional Children and Merrill Education. (2005). *Universal Design for Learning*. Atlanta, GA.

Deiner, Penny Low. (2004). *Resources for Educating Children with Diverse Abilities, 4th Edition*. Florence, KY: Thomson Delmar Learning.

Dieker, Lisa. (2006). *Co-Teaching Lesson Plan Book (Third Edition)*. Whitefish Bay, WI: Knowledge By Design.

Dodge, Judith. (2005). *Differentiation in Action*. Jefferson City, MO: Scholastic Inc.

Elias, Maurice & Linda B. Butler. (2005). *Social Decision Making/Social Problem Solving A Curriculum for Academic, Social and Emotional Learning*. Champaign, IL: Research Press.

Elias, Maurice & Harriett Arnold. (2006). *The Educator's Guide to Emotional Intelligence and Academic Achievement*. Thousand Oaks, CA: Corwin Press.

Ellery, Valerie. (2004). *Creating Strategic Readers*. Newark, DE: International Reading Association.

Elliott, Judy L. & Martha L. Thurlow. (2000). *Improving Test Performance of Students with Disabilities. On District and State Assessments*. Thousand Oaks, CA: Corwin Press.

Ewy, Christine. (2003). *Teaching with Visual Frameworks*. Thousand Oaks, CA: Corwin Press.

Friedlander, Brian S. (2005). *Assistive Technology: A Way to Differentiate Instruction for Students with Disabilities*. (video) Port Chester, NY: National Professional Resources, Inc.

Friend, Marilyn. (2004). *The Power of Two: Making a Difference Through Co-Teaching, 2nd Edition* (Video). Bloomington, IN: Forum on Education.

Fry, Edward & J. Kress. (2006). *The Reading Teacher's Book of Lists*. San Francisco, CA: Jossey-Bass.

Fuchs, D., Mock, D., Morgan, P., & Young, C. (2003). *Responsiveness-to-intervention: Definitions, evidence, and implications for learning disabilities construct*. Learning Disabilities: Research and Practice, 18(3), 157-171.

Fuchs, L. (2003). *Assessing intervention responsiveness: conceptual and technical issues*. Learning Disabilities Research & Practice, 18(3), 172-186.

Ganske, Kathy. (2006). *Word Sorts & More*. New York, NY: The Guilford Press.

Gardner, Howard. (1996). *How Are Kids Smart?* (Video) Port Chester, NY: National Professional Resources, Inc.

Gold, Mimi. (2003). *Help for the Struggling Student: Ready-to-Use Strategies and Lessons to Build Attention, Memory, and Organizational Skills*. San Francisco, CA: Jossey-Bass.

Goleman, Daniel. (1996). *Emotional Intelligence: A New Vision for Educators* (Video). Port Chester, NY: National Professional Resources, Inc.

Good, R.H. & Kaminski, R.A. (2001). *Dynamic indicators of basic early literacy skills* (6th ed.). Eugene, OR: Institute for the Development of Educational Achievement.

Gorman, Jean Cheng. (2001). *Emotional Disorders and Learning Disabilities in the Classroom: Interactions and Interventions.* Thousand Oaks, CA: Corwin Press.

Gregory, Gale & Carolyn Chapman. (2002). *Differentiated Instructional Strategies: One Size Doesn't Fit All.* Thousand Oaks, CA: Corwin Press.

Gresham, F.M. (2001). *Responsiveness to intervention: An alternative approach to the identification of learning disabilities.* Paper presented at the Learning Disabilities Summit, Washington, DC.

Grimes, J., & Kurns, S. (2003, December). *An intervention-based system for addressing NCLB and IDEA expectations: A multiple tiered model to ensure every child learns.* Paper presented at the National Research Center on Learning Disabilities Responsiveness-to-Intervention Symposium, Kansas City, MO.

Gusman, Jo. (2004). *Differentiated Instruction & the English Language Learner: Best Practices to Use With Your Students (K-12)* (Video). Port Chester, NY: National Professional Resources, Inc.

Haager, Diane, J. Klinger, & S. Vaughan. (2007). *Evidence-Based Reading Practices for Response to Intervention.* Baltimore, MD: Paul H. Brookes Publishing Co.

Haager, Diane & J. Dimino. (2007). *Interventions for Reading Success.* Baltimore, MD: Paul H. Brookes Publishing Co.

Heacox, Diane. (2002). *Differentiated Instruction: How to Reach and Teach All Learners (Grades 3-12).* Minneapolis, MN: Free Spirit Press.

Hehir, Thomas. (2005). *New Directions in Special Education.* Cambridge, MA: Harvard University Press.

Hiskes, Dolores G. (2007). *Reading Pathways.* San Francisco, CA: Josey-Bass.

Iervolino, Constance & Helene Hanson. (2003). *Differentiated Instructional Practice Video Series: A Focus on Inclusion (Tape 1), A Focus on the Gifted (Tape 2).* Port Chester, NY: National Professional Resources, Inc.

Jensen, Eric. (2000). *Different Brains, Different Learners: How to Reach the Hard to Reach.* San Diego, CA: The Brain Store.

Jensen, Eric. (2000).*The Fragile Brain: What Impairs Learning and What We Can Do About It.* (Video). Port Chester, NY: National Professional Resources, Inc.

Jensen, Eric. (2000). *Practical Applications of Brain-Based Learning.* (Video). Port Chester, NY: National Professional Resources, Inc.

Kagan, Spencer & Laurie Kagan. (1999). *Reaching Standards Through Cooperative Learning: Providing for ALL Learners in General Education Classrooms* (4-video series). Port Chester, NY: National Professional Resources, Inc.

Kagan, Spencer & Miguel Kagan. (1998). *Multiple Intelligences: The Complete MI Book.* San Clemente, CA: Kagan Cooperative Learning.

Kame'enui, Edward J. & Deborah C. Simmons. (1999). *Adapting Curricular Materials, Volume 1: An Overview of Materials Adaptations—Toward Successful Inclusion of Students with Disabilities: The Architecture of Instruction.* Reston, VA: Council for Exceptional Children.

Katzman, Lauren I. & Allison G. Gandhi (Editors). (2005). *Special Education for a New Century.* Cambridge, MA: Harvard Educational Review.

Kemp, Karen. (2007). *RTI Tackles Reading* (Video). Port Chester, NY: National Professional Resources, Inc.

Kemp, Karen. (2007). *RTI: The Classroom Connection.* Port Chester, NY: Dude Publishing.

Kennedy, Eugene. (2003). *Raising Test Scores for All Students: An Administrator's Guide to Improving Standardized Test Performance.* Thousand Oaks, CA: Corwin Press.

Kleinert, Harold L. & Jacqui F. Kearns. (2001). *Alternate assessment: Measuring Outcomes and Supports for Students with Disabilities.* Baltimore, MD: Brookes Publishing Company, Inc.

Lavoie, Richard. (2005). *Beyond F.A.T. City* (Video). Charlotte, NC: PBS Video.

Lavoie, Richard. (1989). *F.A.T. City: How Difficult Can This Be?* (Video). Charlotte, NC: PBS Video.

Lavoie, Richard.(2005). *It's So Much Work to Be Your Friend* (Video). Charlotte, NC: PBS Video.

Levine, Mel. (2002). *A Mind at a Time.* New York, NY: Simon & Schuster.

Lickona, Thomas. (2004). *Character Matters.* New York, NY: Touchstone.

Long, Nicholas, & William Morse. (1996). *Conflict in the Classroom: The Education of At-Risk and Troubled Students, 5th Edition.* Austin, TX: Pro-Ed, Inc.

Maanum, Jody L. (2003). *The General Educator's Guide to Special Education, 2nd Edition.* Minnetonka, MN: Peytral Publications, Inc.

Moll, Anne M. (2003). *Differentiated Instruction Guide for Inclusive Teaching.* Port Chester, NY: Dude Publishing.

Moskal, Mary Kay & C. Blachowicz. (2006). *Partnering for Fluency.* New York, NY: The Guilford Press.

Munk, Dennis D. (2003). *Solving the Grading Puzzle for Students with Disabilities.* Whitefish Bay, WI: Knowledge by Design, Inc.

National Association of State Directors of Special Education (NASDSE). (2005). *Response to Intervention: Policy, Considerations, and Implementation.* Alexandria, VA: NASDSE.

Nelsen, Jane, Lynn Lott & H. Stephen Glenn. (2000). *Positive Discipline In The Classroom: Developing Mutual Respect, Cooperation, and Responsibility in Your Classroom.* Three Rivers, MI: Three Rivers Press.

Nolet, Victor & Margaret McLaughlin. (2000). *Accessing the General Curriculum: Including Students with Disabilities in Standards-Based Reform.* Thousand Oaks, CA: Corwin Press.

Norlander, Karen. (2006). *RTI Tackles the LD Explosion: A Good IDEA Becomes Law (Video).* Port Chester, NY: National Professional Resources, Inc.

O'Connor, Rollanda, & A. Notari-Syverson. (2005). *Ladders to Literacy.* Baltimore, MD: Paul H. Brookes Publishing Co.

O'Connor, Rollanda. (2007). *Teaching Word Recognition.* New York, NY: The Guilford Press.

Purcell, Sherry & Debbie Grant. (2004). *Using Assistive Technology to Meet Literacy Standards.* Verona, WI: IEP Resources.

Reider, Barbara. (2005). *Teach More and Discipline Less.* Thousand Oaks, CA: Corwin Press.

Renzulli, Joseph S. (1999). *Developing the Gifts and Talents of ALL Students: The Schoolwide Enrichment Model* (Video). Port Chester, NY: National Professional Resources, Inc.

Rief, Sandra F. (1998). *The ADD/ADHD Checklist.* Paramus, NJ: Prentice Hall.

Rief, Sandra F. (2004). *ADHD & LD: Powerful Teaching Strategies & Accommodations* (Video). Port Chester, NY: National Professional Resources, Inc.

Rief, Sandra F. & Julie A. Heimburge. (1996). *How to Reach & Teach All Students in the Inclusive Classroom: Ready-To-Use Strategies, Lessons, and Activities for Teaching Students with Learning Needs.* West Nyack, NY: Center for Applied Research in Education.

Rose, D. & A. Meyer (Editors). (2002). *Teaching Every Student in the Digital Age.* Alexandria, VA: ASCD.

Rose, D. & A. Meyer (Editors). (2005). *The Universally Designed Classroom: Accessible Curriculum and Digital Technologies.* Cambridge, MA: Harvard University Press.

Rutherford, Paula. (2002). *Instruction for All Students.* Alexandria, VA: Just Ask Publications.

Salovey, Peter. (1998). *Optimizing Intelligences: Thinking, Emotion, and Creativity* (Video). Port Chester, NY: National Professional Resources, Inc.

Shaywitz, Sally. (2003). *Overcoming Dyslexia: A New and Complete Science-Based Program for Reading Problems at Any Level.* New York, NY: Knopf Publishing.

Shinn, M. (1989). *Curriculum-based measurement: Assessing special children.* New York: Guilford Press.

Shumm, Jeanne Shay. (1999). *Adapting Curricular Materials, Volume 2: Kindergarten Through Grade Five—Adapting Reading & Math Materials for the Inclusive Classroom.* Reston, VA: Council for Exceptional Children.

Shumm, Jeanne Shay. (2006). *Reading Assessment and Instruction for All Learners.* New York, NY: The Guilford Press.

Snell, Martha E. & Rachel Janney. (2000). *Collaborative Teaming.* Baltimore, MD: Paul H. Brookes Publishing Co., Inc.

Snell, Martha E. & Rachel Janney. (2000). *Social Relationships & Peer Support.* Baltimore, MD: Paul H. Brookes Publishing Co., Inc.

Sousa, David A. (2001). *How the Special Needs Brain Learns.* Thousand Oaks, CA: Corwin Press.

Starrett, Edmund V. (2007). *Teaching Phonics for Balanced Reading.* Thousand Oaks, CA: Corwin Press.

Strichart, Stephen S., Charles T. Mangrum II & Patricia Iannuzzi. (1998). *Teaching Study Skills* and Strategies to Students with Learning Disabilities, Attention Deficit Disorders, *or Special Needs, 2nd Edition.* Boston, MA: Allyn & Bacon, 1998.

Thompson, Sandra, Rachel Quenemeen, Martha Thurlow, & James Ysseldyke. (2001). *Alternate Assessments for Students with Disabilities.* Thousand Oaks, CA: Corwin Press.

Thurlow, Martha L., Judy L. Elliott & James E. Ysseldyke. (1998). *Testing Students with Disabilities: Practical Strategies for Complying With District and State Requirements.* Thousand Oaks, CA: Corwin Press.

Tilton, Linda. (2003). *Teacher's Toolbox for Differentiating Instruction: 700 Strategies, Tips, Tools, & Techniques.* Shorewood, MN: Covington Cove Publications.

Tomlinson, Carol Ann. (2001). *How to Differentiate Instruction in Mixed-Ability Classrooms, 2nd Edition.* Alexandria, VA: ASCD.

Tracey, Diane & L. Mandel-Morrow. (2006). *Lenses on Reading.* New York, NY: The Guilford Press.

Villa, Richard A. & Jacqueline S. Thousand. (2004). *A Guide to Co-Teaching.* Thousand Oaks, CA: Corwin Press.

Watson, T. Steuart & Mark W. Steege. (2003). *Conducting School-Based Functional Behavioral Assessments: A Practitioner's Guide.* New York, NY: Guilford Press.

Wormel, Rick. *(2006). Fair Isn't Always Equal. Portland*, ME: Stenhouse Publishers.

Wright, Jim. (2007). *RTI Toolkit.* Port Chester, NY: Dude Publishing.

Support Statements/Testimonials

We started using Patricia Oelwein's methodology when our son, Marc, was three years old. It is a user-friendly, easy to follow approach that made reading a fun, family affair. Marc not only learned to read, but his verbal skills also increased: as he became able to read longer sentences, he also spoke in longer sentences.

Children who have Down syndrome are visual learners and the Oelwein method is based on whole word sight recognition as opposed to a phonics approach. Reading was Marc's main academic strength when he started school. While some classmates couldn't read or even recognize their own names, Marc was already reading 100 words. Reading improved his self-confidence and he was proud to help other students who were struggling with the reading process.

Reading is still an enjoyable pastime for Marc. Besides books, he reads the sports section, the weather page and the comics in the newspaper. He enjoys pointing out comical billboard signs and advertisements.

He has done classroom presentations reading from cue cards and he has participated in plays and memorized speeches. Now, at age 14, reading continues to play an important part in his life and has allowed him to participate meaningfully through his years at school.

— Nancy Ceci, Parent
Past President, Toronto Down Syndrome Association
Toronto, Ontario

I used the techniques in Patricia's first book, *Teaching Reading to Children with Down Syndrome*, to teach my son, who has autism, to read. We started with important sight words, the Dolch words, and lastly phonics. He is in Grade 2 now and reads at level for his age. This effective program can be delivered easily in a home-based environment or in collaboration with your school.

— Cecilia Vespa
Waterdown, Ontario

During the years that I was privileged to teach children with special needs, Patricia Oelwein's program was the most rewarding and successful of the many learning strategies I attempted. Specific elements were critical to this success. Teaching in a way that was meaningful, interesting and relevant to the student's world was central to the goals of the program. Consistent implementation and closely following the strategies of the program was key. All children do not learn at the same rate, so equally important was perseverance.

With one of my students, Melody, it took eighteen months of ongoing use of this program before she was able to transfer her ability to discriminate words to other forms of print materials. Perseverance had paid off and there was no stopping her.

By adapting the technique to modify her program in an integrated setting, Melody was exposed to a more enhanced learning experience. She had language delays, but through reading, her articulation and verbal skills progressed dramatically. With success in reading came improved self-esteem, behavior, confidence and independence. Most importantly, Melody saw herself as a learner and so did her classmates.

Opportunities to read quickly became the best motivator for Melody to complete tasks. She absolutely loved books and reading enriched her life by becoming her favorite activity.

Without perseverance and consistently following the program's techniques in an interesting and meaningful way for Melody, these gains would not have been possible. The satisfaction and pleasure of participating in this program and the rewards it provided for Melody, remain one of my most significant and rewarding experiences in teaching.

— Carol Herbert
Teacher

About the Authors

Leslie Todd Broun, M.Ed.

Leslie Broun is presently Project Manager for the Geneva Centre for Autism in Toronto, Ontario, training teaching assistants to work with students with ASD. Previously, Leslie was the Special Programs Consultant for students with Autism Spectrum Disorders for the Peel District School Board in Mississauga, Ontario. Over the past twenty years, she has worked with students who have ASD both in self-contained and mainstream settings, and has been a teaching instructor and presenter at workshops and conferences in Canada and internationally. Her primary professional focuses have been the development of practical and effective learning strategies and materials for teaching academic skills to students with ASD and other developmental disabilities, as well as the development of perspectives on inclusion and curriculum modification.

Patricia Logan Oelwein, M.Ed.

Patricia Oelwein, a consultant in private practice, worked at the University of Washington in the Down Syndrome Programs at the Center on Human Development and Disabilities for twenty-five years. The positions she held in the program include teacher in demonstration classrooms, coordinator, and outreach trainer. She has provided specialized training for teaching children with Down syndrome and other developmental delays throughout the United States and in twelve other countries spanning six continents.

Ms. Oelwein has published research articles and instructional materials, edited *Advances in Down Syndrome* with Valentine Dmitriev, and wrote *Teaching Reading to Children with Down Syndrome* and *Al Nahada Functional Assessment with Applied Academics.*

Since 1991 she has been consultant to the Al Nahada Model Schools in Riyadh, KSA. Ms. Oelwein considers this project her greatest professional accomplishment.